EMAIL "Messages"

EMAIL "Messages"

*A Minister Responds to Questions
from His Congregation*

STEVEN A. CRANE

RESOURCE *Publications* • Eugene, Oregon

EMAIL "MESSAGES"
A Minister Responds to Questions from His Congregation

Copyright © 2011 Steven A. Crane. All rights reserved. Except for brief quotations in critical publications or reviews, no part of this book may be reproduced in any manner without prior written permission from the publisher. Write: Permissions, Wipf and Stock Publishers, 199 W. 8th Ave., Suite 3, Eugene, OR 97401.

Resource Publications
An Imprint of Wipf and Stock Publishers
199 W. 8th Ave., Suite 3
Eugene, OR 97401

www.wipfandstock.com

ISBN 13: 978-1-61097-496-7

Manufactured in the U.S.A.

CONTENTS

Preface / ix

Questions about God
1. Is Belief in God Irrational? / 3
2. Who Made God? / 5
3. What Is the Special Name of God? / 7
4. How Can a Loving God Send People to Hell? / 9
5. Is the God of the Old Testament Different than the God of the New Testament? / 12
6. Isn't the Belief in the Trinity Contradictory? / 14
7. Do You Really Believe in Miracles? / 17

Questions about Christ
8. How Do You Know that Jesus Even Existed? / 21
9. Did Jesus Really Claim to Be God? / 23
10. Did Jesus Really Die on the Cross? / 26
11. Did Jesus Really Rise Again? / 28
12. Was Jesus Really Dead Three Days? / 30
13. Did Jesus Really Preach in Hell? / 31
14. Are the Genealogies of Jesus Contradictory? / 36
15. Did Jesus Have Brothers and Sisters? / 38
16. Is the Shroud of Turin Authentic? / 40
17. Is Jesus Currently Alone in Heaven with God? / 41

Questions about the Bible

18. What Is the Bible? / 45
19. Can You Give Me the Message of the Bible in a Nutshell? / 49
20. Is the Bible to Be Taken Literally or Figuratively? / 51
21. What Evidence Do You Have That the Bible Is Accurate? / 53
22. Has the Bible Been Corrupted? / 56
23. Is the King James Version the Only Authorized Version? / 58
24. What Bible Translation Should I Use? / 64
25. What about the Gospel of Thomas? / 67
26. What about Apocryphal Books? / 69
27. What is the Jesus Seminar? / 71
28. Shouldn't We Expect More Bible? / 73

Questions about Salvation

29. Can I Be a Christian If I've Got Doubts? / 77
30. Can You Lose Your Salvation? / 79
31. What Is the Unpardonable Sin? / 81
32. What about Those Who Have Never Heard the Gospel? / 83
33. What Is Universalism? / 86
34. What about Infant Baptism? / 89
35. What Is the Proper Age for Baptism? / 92
36. What Is the Proper Mode of Baptism? / 94
37. What Is the Purpose of Mortal Life? / 96

Bible Questions

38. What about the Frequency of Communion? / 101
39. What Is the Meaning of Communion? / 103
40. What about the Ten Commandments? / 105

41. What about Tithing? / 107

42. What Is Expository Preaching? / 109

43. What about Cremation? / 111

44. Is Suicide Unforgivable? / 113

45. What about Guardian Angels? / 115

46. What about Other Inhabited Worlds? / 117

Bible Difficulties

47. Where Did Cain Get His Wife? / 121

48. What Is the Mark of Cain? / 123

49. Why Aren't Dinosaurs Mentioned in the Bible? / 125

50. If God Hardened Pharaoh's Heart, Did He Have Free Will? / 127

51. What Are the Nephilim? / 128

52. Is Sunday the Sabbath? / 132

53. What about Modern-day Apostles? / 134

54. What about Spiritual Gifts? / 136

55. What about Homosexuality? / 138

Questions about Eschatology (The End Times)

56. What about the Battle of Armageddon? / 143

57. What about the Antichrist? / 145

58. When Are the Last Days? / 147

59. What Is the Tribulation? / 149

60. What about the Rapture? / 151

61. What Is the Mark of the Beast? / 153

62. What Is the Millennium? / 155

63. Are There Warning Signs of the End of Time? / 157

64. When Do People Go to Heaven? / 159

Objections to Christianity
65. Aren't All Religions Basically the Same? / 163
66. What about All of Christianity's Injustice? / 165
67. Isn't Christianity Narrow-minded? / 168
68. Isn't Religion Culturally Conditioned? / 170
69. Isn't Sincerely Believing Enough? / 172
70. What about the Problem of Evil? / 174

Bibliography / 177

PREFACE

Fifteen years ago, I had the privilege of planting Eagle Christian Church. From humble beginnings in my living room, the church has since grown significantly. During that time I discovered an interesting correlation: as the congregation grew—so did the number of questions I received—some through snail mail, some voice mail, but primarily through email.

About two years ago, I realized that many of the questions I was being asked, I had been asked before—and had previously answered (at least once). Upon this realization, I searched frantically in my file cabinets and on my computer to see if I had stored any of my previous correspondence. I found very little. "Oh," I thought, "if I had only saved the questions and answers in an electronic format!"

Since that time, the questions have continued to come in, and this present work began to take shape as I have faithfully attempted to respond to each—and faithfully saved them as well. These pages are primarily a compilation of answers to questions I have received from folks within the community of believers at Eagle Christian Church.

In keeping with the original genre of the writing (email messages), I have intentionally tried to keep my answers brief and to the point. Understand that with brevity often comes incompleteness. There is always much more that could be said, and often there are many different ways one might attempt to answer a particular question. I have tried to include Bible passages and other resources to help the reader to gain more complete answers to their questions when necessary.

My prayer is that this "question and answer" format will help you on your journey to be able to defend your faith. I believe, as a minister, one of my primary tasks is to equip people with tools necessary to help them answer not only their own questions, but to help them provide answers for others as well. For Scripture tells us, "But in your hearts set apart Christ as Lord. Always be prepared to give an answer to everyone who asks you to give the reason for the hope that you have. But do this with gentleness and respect" (1 Peter 3:15).

Steven A. Crane

Section One

Questions about God

Part One

Questions about God

EMAIL "Messages"

✉ INBOX [1/70]

To: Dr. Crane [eaglechristianchurch.com]
Subject: Is Belief in God Irrational?

---Original Message---

What should I say to my atheist friend who doesn't believe in God because "faith is irrational"?

Reply:

While it is true that atheists don't believe in God, the Bible tells us that God doesn't believe in atheists! The question is: who are you going to believe? While this answer might seem a little sarcastic, the truth is that whether you believe in God or don't believe in God—both are systems of faith! The question is not whether "faith" is irrational, but if our faith is "irrationally placed."

I actually believe it takes far more faith to be an atheist than it does to believe in God. Let me say that even more strongly. Atheism is an untenable position. You might respond to your friend, "I don't have enough faith to be an atheist," and see what kind of reaction that gets. Atheism is a belief system—usually held, not for intellectual reasons, but for moral ones.

The word atheist comes from the Greek word "*atheos*." "*Theos*" is the word for God. "*A*" is a negative particle. Placed together, "*atheos*" literally means "no God." Therefore, an atheist makes this faith claim: there is no God.

Let me demonstrate why that belief system is untenable. Imagine for a moment a circle the size of a common car steering wheel which represents all knowledge: past, present, and future. Let that circle represent everything that is, can, and will ever be known.

Now, take a moment to shade in the portion of that circle that represents how much of "all-knowledge" you possess. Even the brightest among us dare only make a pin-prick on that circle before we appear arrogant. The point is easily demonstrated: there is far more that we don't know than we do know.

I would ask the atheist if it is possible that God resides outside the boundaries of their knowledge. Is it? Which is more rational, to state that you KNOW there is no God, or to say that within the amount of knowledge you possess—you have no knowledge of God? Actually, the atheist would be better served by calling himself an "agnostic"—he has no knowledge of God.

While I cannot prove the existence of God, neither can the atheist prove the nonexistence of God. We can, however, demonstrate that belief in God is not irrational.

For further study see: *I Don't Have Enough Faith to be an Atheist*, by Norman Geisler and Frank Turek.

EMAIL "Messages"

✉ INBOX [2/70]

To: Dr. Crane [eaglechristianchurch.com]
Subject: Who Made God?

---Original Message---

I've heard it said that everything needs a cause. If that is true, then what caused God?

Reply:

I hear this argument often. Philosophers call this the Principle of Sufficient Reason. We use it every day—it is common sense. If you saw a little puppy that did not belong to you suddenly appear in your living room, no one in your family would say, "Hi, puppy. You came from nowhere, didn't you?" No, you would likely look around to try to determine how it got in, and where it came from. You might be unable to find all the answers to your questions, but still you can know with certainty that the puppy came from somewhere—it didn't come from nowhere.

That is the principle to which you refer. But the principle should not be quoted as saying, "Everything needs a cause." The principle needs to be stated, "Everything that has a *beginning* needs a cause." Every finite, contingent thing needs a cause. But God is neither finite nor is he contingent upon anything or anyone. In other words, God does not have a beginning, or a cause—because God is infinite. God is the "uncaused" cause of all finite things. The very word for God used in Scripture is the "I Am"—the always existent one.

If God were finite, your question would be valid—God would need a cause. If God needed a cause, we would then have a problem and would need to look to a point before God existed and then ask, "Who created God?" But that wouldn't solve our problem, it would only intensify it. We would then need to ask, "Who created the one that created God?" This would lead us into a quagmire of "preceding causes."

As it is, we can't ask, "Who caused God?" because God is infinite. You can't go back any farther than that. If you understand this argument, this becomes a powerful argument FOR God rather than an argument against God, because everything that had a beginning needs a cause. Where did the stuff come from that caused stuff? Without God as part of the equation, you will find yourself in a logistical quagmire.

EMAIL "Messages"

✉ INBOX [3/70]

To: Dr. Crane [eaglechristianchurch.com]
Subject: What Is the Special Name of God?

---Original Message---

I have been told that in the Old Testament, Israel knew God by a special name. What is that name?

Reply:

It is true that in the Old Testament, the Israelites knew God by a special name. This name was so special, so holy, that by the time of Jesus (and perhaps for centuries before that), no one said it out loud. The one exception was made when the high priest, once a year, would pronounce the name in the Holy of Holies.

Since Hebrew script originally used only consonants, we can't even be sure how the name was meant to be pronounced: the consonants are YHWH. The best guess is that it was pronounced "Yahweh." Orthodox Jews to this day won't speak this name—they refer only to "the Name" (*HaShem*).

Like most ancient names, YHWH had a meaning. It meant "existence," the "I am who I am," or "I will be who I will be." The name "God" suggests "the uncreated existent one."

Because God's personal name was not to be spoken, the Israelites developed a technique for avoiding doing so when they read Scripture. When they came to the word YHWH, they would say "ADONAI" (which means Lord) instead. To remind themselves to do this, they would write the consonants of YHWH with the vowels of ADONAI. This has brought confusion to later readers who try to say the two words (God and Lord) together. It would look like this. YaHoWaH—a nonsense word, but a reminder not to pronounce the name of God. It also needs to be noted that later generations wrote "Y" as "J," and "W" as "V." When we insert these new letters into the name for God (JHVH) with the vowels of the name for Lord (a-o-a), we get the following made-up word: JaHoVaH, or Jehovah.

Almost all English translations of the Old Testament have continued the practice of discouraging people from pronouncing God's personal name. Instead, where the word YHWH appears, they will insert the word "Lord" usually in small capitals (Lord).

EMAIL "Messages"

✉ INBOX [4/70]

To: Dr. Crane [eaglechristianchurch.com]
Subject: How Can a Loving God Send People to Hell?

---Original Message---

It seems to me that the Bible makes two contradictory statements: that God is a God of love and a God of wrath. How could a loving God send a person to hell?

Reply:

I'm not sure I agree with your basic premise (that love and wrath are contradictory), or your conclusion (that God sends people to hell). Let me attempt to explain both.

First, in my mind, love and wrath are not incompatible—in fact, they are often intertwined. I believe there is a direct correlation between how deeply we love someone and the extent to which we might get angry with them.

Imagine for a moment a close friend who was battling some self-destructive behavior or addiction which was ruining their life (and the lives of others around them). Would you sit by indifferently? I doubt it—not if they were a close friend. You would be angry at them. You would confront them. You would not be afraid to offend them by passing judgment on their destructive behavior.

The greater our love for someone, the greater potential for anger at what is destructive in their lives. As parents, we are often full of both love and anger. It is not contradictory—it happens all the time and at precisely the same time. When our kids are involved in a potentially destructive activity, it is not unloving to respond—it is necessary! If love and anger can reside in the life of a good parent, should we not expect God to exhibit both as well?

In the case of a parent, we might define this type of wrath as: settled opposition and hatred of that which is destroying what we love. In God's case, his anger flows from his love of his creation. God gets angry at injustice, greed, self-centeredness, and evil—precisely because they are destructive to what he loves. God will not (and cannot) tolerate anything or anyone responsible for destroying the creation and the people he loves so dearly. God's wrath stems directly from his love.

Second, I disagree that God "sends" people to hell (I believe in both heaven and hell). God loves everyone and does not want anyone to perish, but all to come to repentance (2 Peter 3:9). God loved the world so much that he sent his one and only son to die, so that whoever believes in him would not perish but have eternal life (John 3:16).

But as a loving God, he does not force himself on anyone. Remember our illustration of a friend struggling with an addiction. After trying and trying and trying to help your friend, there may be a point where you would give up on your friend and say, "If you continue to choose this path, I can no longer help you. But if you come to the point where you are willing to make a change, I will do everything I can to help." This type of action is called "tough love."

Is it possible that this describes God's offer of help to all, but the rejection of his help by some? In other words, God doesn't send a person to hell, but releases them to follow the course of their own actions.

Some have suggested that God simply gives you the life you want—on into eternity. From the Christian perspective, if you want to live with God forever, God has made that option available through his Son, Jesus Christ. But, if you want to be your own person, your own savior, your own lord, and live life without God—you can choose that path for eternity as well.

According to Romans chapter one, God lets people have what they want most—and hell is simply serving yourself—forever. Hell is God giving you the life you want, on into eternity!

EMAIL "Messages"

✉ INBOX [5/70]

To: Dr. Crane [eaglechristianchurch.com]
Subject: Is the God of the Old Testament Different than the God of the New Testament?

---Original Message---

Isn't there a conflict between the harsh and cruel God of the Old Testament and the loving God we read about in the New Testament?

Reply:

The same loving God is spoken of in both the Old and New Testament. The Psalmist writes that "The Lord is gracious and compassionate, slow to anger and rich in love. The Lord is good to all; he has compassion on all he has made" (Psalms 145:8–9). Furthermore, God says in Malachi, "I the Lord do not change" (3:6).

While it is true that the Old Testament contains more stories of God's judgment (cf. the flood, Sodom and Gomorrah, the Sons of Korah, etc.) than the New Testament, God is said to be both loving and holy throughout the Bible.

You might ponder two points. First, the Old Testament covers a period of about four thousand years; the New Testament covers less than one hundred. Second, God is as serious about sin in the New Testament as he was in the past. The New Testament tells of a time when God's judgment will come upon all who have not accepted Christ. Using the Old Testament account of the flood, Peter writes, "They deliberately forget that long ago by God's word . . . the world of that time was deluged and destroyed. By the same word the present heavens and earth are reserved for fire, being kept for the day of judgment and the destruction of ungodly men" (2 Peter 3:5–7).

EMAIL "Messages"

✉ INBOX [6/70]

To: Dr. Crane [eaglechristianchurch.com]
Subject: Isn't the Belief in the Trinity Contradictory?

---Original Message---

Isn't the very doctrine of the Trinity contradictory?

Reply:

The first thing we should probably acknowledge is that the word "Trinity" appears nowhere in the Bible, and yet the concept is inescapable. Christians knowingly use the word to try to make sense of what is taught in Scripture. Having clarified that, I need also admit—I struggle with the doctrine of the Trinity (the tri-unity of God), while firmly believing that it is both scriptural and rational. On the surface, it would seem that God must be one and not three, or conversely, three and not one—but how could God be both three and one at the same time? The very idea seems at first blush to be a violation of the most fundamental law of thought—the law of noncontradiction.

But a closer examination shows that a Christian belief in unity of "three persons" in "one God" is not a contradiction. A contradiction occurs when something is both "A" and "not A" at the same time and in the same sense. God is both three and one at the same time, but not in the same sense. God is three persons, but one in essence. God is three persons, but only one in nature.

It would be a contradiction to say that God had three natures in one nature, or that God was three persons in one person. But it is not a contradiction to claim that God has three persons in one nature.

I have heard many helpful (and yet still lacking) explanations. For example: God is like a triangle. At the same time it has three distinct corners and yet it is only one triangle. With a scalene triangle, each corner is not the same as either of the other corners, or the same as the triangle as a whole, but it is a part of the whole triangle. They are distinct and different, but the same.

Or, for the mathematicians among us, maybe God is like "one to the third power" (1^3), $1 \times 1 \times 1 = 1$. One thing is for sure, God is not $1 + 1 + 1 = 3$, which is tritheism or polytheism. God is one God—completely, simultaneously, congruently in three distinct persons. God is: Father, Son, and Holy Spirit.

Another illustration of the Trinity uses man (formed in God's image) as an example: man is body, mind, and spirit. There is obvious unity between them, yet they are distinct from each other. (This is not to suggest that God is a "person" in the same way we are persons.)[1]

I have heard other examples as well. Water takes three forms: vapor, liquid, and ice. Eggs contain three parts: white, shell, and yolk. The problem with all of these illustrations is that they fall short of providing an adequate explanation. If I'm honest (and I try to be), the Trinity goes beyond any explanation I can give it. It goes beyond reason without going against reason. It can be apprehended, but not fully comprehended. I believe in the Trinity, not because I understand it, but because it is biblical.

If I thought it would help, I would give an explanation of the differences in thought between those who hold an ontological view of

---

1. I am not suggesting that God is a person in the same sense as we are persons. It is intended to indicate three modes of being (subsistence) within the Godhead that are distinct and distinguishable, but not separate or separatable. When we speak of God's "being," or "existence," or "personhood," it can only be by way of analogy. In reality, God is like nothing else in the universe. God's reality is eternal, uncaused, and necessary. To apply these types of terms (being, existence, personhood) to God who stands outside of time and space will always fall short.

the Trinity and those who hold an economic view of the Trinity—but I'm not even sure which one I hold.

Someone once said, "If we try to understand God completely, we may lose our mind. But if we do not believe in the Trinity, we may very well lose our soul."

Scriptural references: Matthew 1:21-23; 3:3 (Isaiah 40:3 of God), 16-17; 11:25; 12:31; 16:16-17; 17:5; 28:18-20; Mark 1:9-11; 2:7-10; 12:36-37; 14:33; 15:39; Luke 1:30-35; 3:21-22; John 1:1-3, 14, 18; 3:16, 18; 5:21-26; 8:24, 28, 58; 10:30; 11:25; 14:1, 9-10, 16; 16:15; 17:5, 21-23; 20:28, 31; Acts 2:21 (Joel 2:32 of Jesus), 33-36, 38; 5:3-9; 7:59; 10:36; Romans 5:1-5; 8:9-11; 9:5; 15:6, 30; 1 Corinthians 1:24; 2:4-16; 3:16-17; 6:11, 19-20; 8:6; 12:4-6; 16:22; 2 Corinthians 1:20-21; 3:17; 5:19; 12:8; 13:14; Galatians 1:1; 3:20; 4:4-6; Ephesians 1:22; 2:18; 3:14-17; 4:4-6; Philippians 2:5-11; Colossians 1:3-8, 15-17 (Psalms 89:27 calls the Messiah the "first-born," i.e. highest of all kings); 2:9; 1 Thessalonians 3:11-12; 5:18-19; 2 Thessalonians 2:13-14; Titus 1:3; 2:13; 3:4-6; Hebrews 1:1-4, 5-10 (Psalms 45:6-7); 8:58; 9:14; 10:30; 13:8; 1 Peter 1:1-2; Jude 20-21; 1 John 4:13-16; 5:20-21; Revelation 1:4, 8; 3:13; 4:8; 5:8-13; 17:14; 19:16; 21:5-6; 22:1-5, 13.

EMAIL "Messages"

✉ INBOX [7/70]

To: Dr. Crane [eaglechristianchurch.com]
Subject: Do You Really Believe in Miracles?

---Original Message---

I believe in God and most of the Bible, but I have trouble with the miracles. Its seems illogical to believe that Jesus could walk on water. Do you really believe the miracles of the Bible?

Reply:

If you believe in God, it is only logical to believe in miracles! To demonstrate this, I would love to ask you three questions. First, is your God able to act? Second, if he is able to act, what do you call acts of God? Third, from our perspective, wouldn't all acts of God be miracles? Logically, miracles are only impossible if there is no God.

I'd like to tell you a fable. In order for this story to work, you need to pretend inanimate objects and animals can talk. A dog and a hunter were out by a tree near a lake on a warm, fall day. The dog was resting under the tree when the hunter called for the dog to come. The tree said to the dog, "You can't go over there, it's impossible." For the tree to get up and walk—that would be impossible. But the dog got up and walked over to the hunter (there is nothing problematic about a walking dog).

The man told the dog, "I am going to get a gun, load it with ammunition, and shoot some dinner out of the sky." The dog said, "You can't shoot something out of the sky." But the man got up, loaded his rifle, and shot a duck. For the dog—that would have been impossible, but not for the man (there is nothing problematic about a man loading and shooting a gun).

Unfortunately, the duck landed in the middle of the lake. It would be possible for either the man or the dog to swim out to retrieve the duck, but no one would suggest they walk across the top of the water—that would be impossible. But for God, who created the water, there is nothing problematic about it.

If there is a God, why can't he walk on water, heal the sick, make the lame walk, give sight to the blind, cure the leper, multiply fish and loaves, and make wine from water (just to name a few)? For man, these are all impossibilities. But none are problematic if there is a God. Actually, it is only logical that if there is a God, he could in fact do these things and more. Miracles are only miracles from man's perspective, not from the vantage point of God.

All the above mentioned events pale in comparison to the most significant miracle in the history of the world—the resurrection of Jesus Christ from the dead. Without it, Christianity offers no hope. But again, there is no reason to dismiss it. God is the one who created life, he can certainly restore it. It is precisely because of the resurrection of Jesus Christ that I am a Christian and believe in God. I believe in God because he has acted miraculously and revealed himself in history through his Son Jesus Christ and his Word.

Section Two

Questions about Christ

EMAIL "Messages"

✉ INBOX [8/70]

To: Dr. Crane [eaglechristianchurch.com]
Subject: How Do You Know that Jesus Even Existed?

---Original Message---

How do you know that Jesus even existed?

Reply:

I know of no reputable scholar who would deny that Jesus is an actual historical figure. Still, let me try to answer your question.

First, the Bible has been proven to be a reliable historical record. The New Testament's central figure is the person of Jesus Christ.

Second, there are at least thirty-nine sources outside of the Bible that attest to nearly one hundred facts regarding Jesus' life. These sources included the Roman historian Tacitus, the *Didache* (early Christian writings), Pliny the Younger, Suetonius, etc. Let me mention one highly recognized historian of the time who attests to the life of Jesus. First-century Flavius Josephus affirms that Jesus lived and that he performed amazing deeds. He also testifies that Pilate condemned Jesus to die and that he was reportedly seen alive by many after the crucifixion. Maybe even more telling—enemies of Christianity attest to Jesus' life, teachings, crucifixion, and the resurrection.

Third, the *Babylonian Talmud* (a collection of ancient Jewish writings) mentions that Jesus was killed on the eve of Passover.

Fourth, the *Encyclopaedia Britannica* devotes over 20,000 words to the person of Jesus Christ and never once hints that he did not exist.

Finally, even our calendar testifies to the fact that Jesus lived a little over 2000 years ago.

The evidence is secure. There can be no doubt that Jesus of Nazareth was a real person. The only question that remains is what you will do with him.

Recommended reading: *The Case for the Real Jesus*, Lee Strobel.

EMAIL "Messages"

✉ INBOX [9/70]

To: Dr. Crane [eaglechristianchurch.com]
Subject: Did Jesus Really Claim to Be God?

---Original Message---

Did Jesus really claim to be God or was that something that was made up later?

Reply:

Liberal scholars often suggest that Jesus never claimed divinity for himself; instead, the early church fabricated this doctrine after Christ's death. This, however, is not what the evidence shows.

Let me give you seven factors (many more could be put forward) that point toward Jesus as believing he was the one and only Son of God.

First, Jesus claimed divinity when he forgave sins. To the paralytic he said, "Son, your sins are forgiven" (Mark 2:5). The religious leaders understood the implications of this and made accusations against Jesus: "He's blaspheming! Who can forgive sins but God alone?" (2:7). Jesus responded to them by saying, "But that you may know that the Son of Man has authority on earth to forgive sins . . . I tell you, get up, take your mat and go home" (2:10–11).

Second, Jesus claimed divinity when he applied the "I AM" sayings to himself. For example, Jesus says, "I tell you the truth . . . before Abraham was born, I AM" (John 8:58). This was an obvious allusion to God's words to Moses out of the burning bush, and were so unmistakably a declaration of equality with God that the religious leaders picked up rocks to stone him. A quick survey of "I AM" statements in the New Testament (primarily in the Gospel of John) show that Jesus applied a title of deity to himself: I AM the Good Shepherd (10:11); I AM the Bread of Life (6:35); I AM the Light of the Word (8:12; 9:5); I AM the Door (10:7, 9); I AM the Resurrection and the Life (11:23–26); I AM the Way and the Truth and the Life (14:4); I AM the True Vine (15:1). There are also other statements where just the phrase I AM is used by itself.

Third, Jesus claimed divinity when he referred to himself as, "The Son of Man." This is Jesus' favorite self description and he applies it to himself more than four dozen times. While some misunderstand this to be a mere claim of humanity, scholars agree that this is a reference to Daniel, where the Son of Man was ushered into the very presence of the Ancient of Days and: "He was given authority, glory and sovereign power; all peoples, nations and men of every language worshiped him. His dominion is an everlasting dominion that will not pass away, and his kingdom is one that will never be destroyed" (Daniel 7:13–14). The Son of Man was a divine figure in the Old Testament, and by claiming this title he was indeed claiming divinity.

A fourth factor showing that Jesus claimed divinity comes through the way he taught. Jesus believed that the eternal destiny of people hinged on whether they believed in him. "I told you that you would die in your sins; if you do not believe that I am [the one I claim to be], you will indeed die in your sins" (John 8:24). Jesus also said, "I tell you, whoever acknowledges me before men, the Son of Man will also acknowledge him before the angels of God. But he who disowns me before men will be disowned before the angels of God" (Luke 12:8–9). Jesus taught that salvation depended upon their confession of him. Jesus' claim to divinity as he taught is further evidenced in the phrase he commonly employed: "Truly, truly," or "Verily, verily," or "Amen I say to you." These different translations of the same phrase convey this message—"I swear in advance to you the truthfulness of what I am about to say." In Judaism, you needed the testimony of two witnesses to confirm truthfulness. But Jesus witnessed to the truth of his own sayings. He did so by divine authority.

A fifth factor showing that Jesus claimed divinity for himself comes through his use of the Aramaic term "Abba." This reflected intimacy that was absent in ancient Judaism. Devout Jews would not even pronounce the personal name of God out of fear that they might take it in vain. Jesus claimed a personal relationship with God and, thus shed light on how he regarded himself.

Sixth, Jesus claimed divinity through his miracles. Jesus stressed that the signs he performed were a sign of the coming of the kingdom of God: "If I drive out demons by the finger of God, then the kingdom of God has come to you" (Luke 11:20). Although others performed miracles, Jesus did not consider himself simply to be a miracle worker, but the one in whom and through whom the promises of God's kingdom came to pass.

Finally, one last indicator of Jesus' claim to divinity can be seen in his post-resurrection encounter with Thomas. Knowing that Thomas had doubts about the resurrection, Jesus offered him the opportunity to personally check out the evidence for himself. As Thomas looks at Jesus he proclaims, "My Lord and my God" (John 20:28). Jesus' reaction is telling. It would have been blasphemy to have knowingly received Thomas's worship unless Jesus really was God. But Jesus does not rebuke Thomas. Actually, Jesus praises Thomas: "Because you have seen me, you have believed; blessed are those who have not seen and yet have believed" (20:29). In the same way, when Jesus asks Peter, "Who do you say I am?", Peter responds, "You are the Christ, the Son of the living God" (Matthew 16:15–17). Jesus does not try to correct Peter, but affirms that this was revealed to him by God himself.

For further reading: See *Jesus Is the Christ: Studies in the Theology of John*, by Leon Morris.

EMAIL "Messages"

✉ INBOX [10/70]

To: Dr. Crane [eaglechristianchurch.com]
Subject: Did Jesus Really Die on the Cross?

---Original Message---

Isn't it possible that Jesus didn't really die on the cross? Could Jesus have been in a coma and simply resuscitated?

Reply:

Many have certainly made this claim. The Koran, for example, claims that Jesus only pretended to be dead (Surah IV:157). Others have claimed that Jesus was drugged, but revived in the tomb. Still others have suggested (as you have) that Jesus was simply in a coma.

This question is of utmost importance, because if Jesus did not die, there is no significance in a resurrection—it is no miracle for a live man to walk out of a tomb. In order for one to speculate that Jesus "swooned," critics must overcome the preponderance of evidence. Let me give you ten facts as we know them.

1. There is no evidence to suggest that Jesus was drugged. He turned down the common painkiller that was usually given to crucifixion victims (Mark 15:23).

2. The loss of blood makes death highly probable and survival highly improbable (in the garden, from the beatings, the crown of thorns, the nails, the spear).

3. Jesus was beaten and whipped repeatedly by the cat of nine tails (a whip with pieces of bone, rock and pottery). This type

of scourging was often called the "half-death" by Roman soldiers because half of those beaten died from this alone.

4. Jesus suffered five other major wounds: a crown of thorns, three 5–7 inch nails used to secure his hands and feet to the cross, and a spear in his side.

5. The thrust of the spear through the rib cage, pierced Jesus' right lung, the sack around the heart, and the heart itself. This insured that Jesus was dead.

6. The professional executioners did not break Jesus' legs because there was no doubt in their minds about his demise.

7. Jesus was embalmed in nearly 100 pounds of spices. This alone would have killed him. Jesus was then wrapped in bandages from which he could not have escaped.

8. Many hours (parts of three days) were spent in a cold, dark tomb. This would likely have sent Jesus into hypothermia—even if he had somehow survived the events to this point.

9. Pilate asked for assurance that Jesus was really dead.

10. If Jesus merely appeared to witnesses after having been resuscitated, his appearance would not have convinced the world that he was indeed a resurrected Savior.

Add to this list the fact that Jesus himself testified that he was risen from the dead. Are we to conclude that he was lying? All these facts point to the logical and insurmountable conclusion that Jesus truly died for our sins.

EMAIL "Messages"

✉ INBOX [11/70]

To: Dr. Crane [eaglechristianchurch.com]
Subject: Did Jesus Really Rise Again?

---Original Message---

What is the evidence regarding the resurrection of Jesus?

Reply:

Christianity lives or dies with the resurrection. Understanding this, opponents of Christianity have tried to explain away the resurrection by every possible means—to no avail. Here are twelve obstacles critics must overcome in order to deny the resurrection.

1. There was an empty tomb.
2. There were grave clothes lying on the shelf of the tomb, neatly wrapped and folded.
3. Jesus' body could not have been stolen—the tomb was sealed with an official seal and guarded by Roman soldiers.
4. The Jews and Roman authorities had no desire to steal the body, in fact, they wanted it kept in the tomb. Even if they did remove the body, they would have produced it when the disciples began to preach the resurrection.
5. Three women visited the empty tomb. Peter and John also ran to the empty tomb. Even if you suggest they all went to the wrong tomb, why didn't the Roman authorities correct them when they proclaimed the resurrection?
6. Jesus did not merely "swoon" or come out of a coma. If he did, how could he find the strength to unwrap himself, push away

the stone, overpower the Roman guards, walk to Jerusalem on wounded feet, and then convince the world he was "resurrected with power"?

7. The resurrection was evidenced by twelve different post-resurrection appearances by more than 500 people: Mary Magdalene (John 20:11); other women (Matthew 28:9–10); Peter (Luke 24:34); two disciples (Luke 24:13–32); to ten apostles without Thomas (Luke 24:33–49); to the apostles with Thomas (John 20:26–30); to seven apostles in Galilee (John 21); to all the apostles (Mattthew 28:16–20); to all the apostles again (Acts 1:4–9); to 500 people at one time (1 Corinthians 15:6); to James (1 Corinthians 15:7); and to Paul (1 Corinthians 15:7).

8. Thomas was encouraged to touch his hands and feet and to place his fingers in the nail holes and his sword-pierced side.

9. The changed lives of the apostles are proof they saw the resurrected Christ.

10. The apostles' willingness to die for their belief in the resurrection evidences its reality.

11. The growth of the church in Jerusalem immediately following the resurrection.

12. The continued growth of the church throughout the centuries.

The historical evidence is overwhelming in favor of the resurrection—Christ died for our sins, he was buried, and he was resurrected on the third day. His life and teachings have influenced and shaped the world as no other. The evidence validates his claims. He is more than just a great man or a moral teacher; he is the King of Kings and Lord of Lords.

EMAIL "Messages"

✉ INBOX [12/70]

To: Dr. Crane [eaglechristianchurch.com]
Subject: Was Jesus Really Dead Three Days?

---Original Message---

If Jesus was crucified on Friday, how could he have been in the grave three days and nights?

Reply:

Some scholars do believe that Jesus was in the grave for three full days and nights (72 hours). Those who hold to this suggest that he was crucified either on Wednesday or Thursday. In support of their view they posit that Passover was not a fixed day (Friday), but that it floated from year to year. They then point out that the Bible does not record any activity for Jesus on Wednesday—allowing them to move the crucifixion up accordingly.

Most biblical scholars, however, believe that Jesus was crucified on Friday and acknowledge that Jesus was only in the tomb for parts of three days—pointing out that the phrase "on the third day" (Matthew 16:21; 17:23; 20:19; 26:61) can legitimately be understood to mean "within three days," rather than 72 hours. It is certainly used this way elsewhere (cf. Esther 4:16).

This second view certainly fits best within the chronological order of events given by the gospel writers (see Mark 14:1ff) as well as the fact that Jesus died on Passover day (Friday) to fulfill the conditions of being our Passover Lamb (1 Corinthians 5:7; Leviticus 23:5–15).

EMAIL "Messages"

✉ INBOX [13/70]

To: Dr. Crane [eaglechristianchurch.com]
Subject: Did Jesus Really Preach in Hell?

---Original Message---

Did Jesus really go to the depths of hell to preach the gospel to spirits who were held captive there?

Reply:

The question you ask finds its basis in 1 Peter 3:19–20. The great theologian, Martin Luther, said that this section of Scripture was: "... a more obscure passage perhaps than any other in the New Testament," and that he did not know "for a certainty just what Peter means."

No one can come to such a passage with an air of certainty, but that does not mean we cannot wrestle with it. To attempt to understand this passage, a person must ask and answer a number of questions. When did Jesus go and preach? To whom did Jesus preach? What was the message Jesus preached, and what does this illustration of baptism and Noah mean?

There are many opinions, and not all scholars agree. I will give you the most common interpretations, and then my opinion (you are certainly free to disagree).

When did Jesus go and preach? (3:18–19)

Jesus is said to have preached to "spirits in prison." When did this happen? There are three answers given.

1. Some say this happened in the O. T. before Jesus came to earth. Christ's spirit was in Noah as Noah preached to those

imprisoned by sin (but now in hell). Through the preaching of Noah, the spirit of Christ was revealed, but those who heard him preach rejected his message, so they are now in spiritual prison. This is referring back to Genesis, and it was not Christ preaching, but Christ's spirit being preached by Noah.

2. A second view (the most popular) holds that between his death and resurrection, Christ preached to those people who had previously died without hearing the gospel message. During the period when Jesus was in the grave, his spirit went and preached to souls in Hades, giving them an opportunity to hear the gospel.

3. My personal opinion is that this is referring to a post-resurrection appearance. I actually think that the text demands this view. Look at verse 18 a little closer. Christ was put to death in the body but made alive by the Spirit. In Greek this is a contrasting clause. On the one hand—he died. On the other hand—he was made alive. Literally, "On the one hand put to death in the flesh, on the other hand made alive in the spirit. At which time . . ." It is a post resurrection that is in view.

To whom did Jesus preach? (3:19)
Again there are three basic views.

1. The first view holds that Noah preached to men, in the spirit of Christ, who because they were disobedient, are now in prison waiting the resurrection.

2. The second view (most popular) is that during the time in the tomb, Jesus went and preached to "the souls of men" who were disobedient in the Old Testament, giving them the opportunity to hear the gospel.

3. Again, I've got to disagree with both these views. Both these views assume the word "spirit" here refers to the spirit of

men. When the word "spirit" is used in Scripture, it is seldom used of men unless it is qualified by the phrase "the spirit of man." The word "soul" is usually used. Not only that, but again in this passage we find a contrast between verse 19, "the spirits who were disobedient, in prison" and that of verse 22, "those angels, authorities and powers who are in submission to him." These are not the spirits of men, but fallen angels and demonic forces that oppose Christ.

Which brings us to a third, and probably the most important question.

What did Jesus preach?

This is the easiest question to answer. But even here we have two views.

1. The first view (most popular) holds that Christ preached salvation.
2. But the word here translated "preach" is not *euangelion*, to preach the gospel. It is actually the word *karrusso* which means to "proclaim" or "announce." The message proclaimed is the message of victory and triumph—Jesus is alive and well. He has demonstrated victory, power over death. He has triumphed and is proclaiming that victory with finality. The battle has been fought; the victory has been secured.

And notice our text again. These difficult portions are sandwiched between a section that is easily understood. "For Christ died for sins once for all, the righteous for the unrighteous, to bring you to God. He was put to death in the body, but made alive by the Spirit . . . (he) has gone into heaven and is at God's right hand—with angels, authorities and powers in submission to him."

Christ died . . . once for all. The righteous for the unrighteous. To bring you to God. He was put to death . . . but is now alive. Everything is in submission to him. What hope this would have brought to first century Christians, who at times thought they were losing the battle. It's the message of hope, and life, and victory; and this victory was announced by Christ at his resurrection to all spiritual forces who opposed him. God dealt with sin in the past by destroying people with the flood, but in these times, he dealt sin a death blow through the resurrection of Jesus Christ. The message being proclaimed here is victory over death, victory over sin, and victory over our spiritual enemies.

Which brings us to the last question we need to answer.

What does the illustration of baptism mean? (3:21)

Again there are two words I'd like to point out to you.

The word "symbolizes" is the word *anti-topos*. It's a figure, an example, a comparison. And Peter makes sure we know a couple of things about this example. He tells us what baptism is not. It is not a magical or mystical rite. There is no power in the water to save. It's not removal of dirt from the flesh (you can take a bath at home). It's not holy water.

But then he tells us what it is: it's a pledge (we'll come back to that word in a minute) and he tells us where the power is found. "It saves you by the resurrection of Jesus Christ." That's the purpose of this passage—to highlight what Jesus has done, and how he has shown his ultimate victory. Jesus Christ is risen. In Jesus there is victory.

But let's look at that word "pledge" (*eperōtēma*) a little more closely. By the way, it's the only time this word is used in Scripture. It's actually taken from the word "question." Its literal meaning is to answer a question. "To give an answer." I picture this as God asking you this simple question: "Do you really want to be a follower of mine?" or Jesus asking, "Are you really willing to make me your Lord?" In order for Jesus to be our Savior, he must first be our Lord. Are you willing to answer God in the affirmative, "Yes, I want to follow you completely"!

Later, in the first and second century, the word was used in legal contracts. It was like signing your name on the dotted line. It was a promise, a pledge, a signature that you would live by the contract. Baptism is this: count me in. I promise, I pledge, I am willing to give you my answer.

Notice: it's not the payment for sin. That was made by Jesus. It's not the gift offered to us freely—that's grace. But it is the pledge, and the acceptance of the offer.

Peter is saying to them, "Don't you know that there is victory in Christ? And don't you want to accept what he has done for you and pledge your life to him?" You see, in our eagerness to find answers to these difficult questions, we might miss the purpose of this passage.

Read this passage one more time without the controversy, and see clearly the picture that is being painted. The purpose of this passage is simply this: Jesus died once for all to bring you to God. You are saved by the resurrection of Jesus Christ. He has triumphed and gone into heaven. He is now seated at God's right hand. Everything is in submission to him. Jesus died once for all, to bring you to God . . . you are saved by the resurrection of Jesus Christ who has gone into heaven and is at God's right hand. Jesus is in control. Is he in control of you?

EMAIL "Messages"

✉ INBOX [14/70]

To: Dr. Crane [eaglechristianchurch.com]
Subject: Are the Genealogies of Jesus Contradictory?

---Original Message---

In reading the genealogies of Jesus in Matthew 1 and Luke 3, they appear to be contradictory. Is there something here that I don't understand?

Reply:

This is a question that has long perplexed readers of the New Testament. At first glance, it does appear that there is a contradiction because Matthew 1:16 indicates that Jacob is Joseph's father, while Luke 3:23 mentions the name of Heli. The usual practice of a Jewish genealogy is to give the name of the father, grandfather, great-grandfather, and so on (either in an ascending or descending order). When comparing the two, one quickly realizes that the names of the two genealogies are not the same.

The best way to understand this is by realizing that while Joseph was the "legal" father of Jesus, he was not the "actual" father of Jesus (cf. the virgin birth, Matthew 1:20). Matthew traces the line through Joseph's father (Jacob), while Luke traces the line of Jesus through Joseph's father-in-law—the father of Mary (Heli).

Take a close look at Luke's account, and you will see an interesting phrase that you might have previously missed. "He [Jesus] was the son, *so it was thought,* of Joseph" (Luke 3:23). In so doing, Luke reminds us of what he has already told us in chapter 1—that Jesus is not the physical son of Joseph, but only of Mary. Joseph is clearly portrayed not as the literal father, but as the *supposed* father. Luke then proceeds to give us the genealogy of Jesus through Mary's family line.

The purpose of the two genealogies is to demonstrate that Jesus was in the complete sense a descendant of David. Through his "legal" father he inherited the royal line, but more importantly, through his mother he was also flesh and blood of King David. Jesus had the proper human credentials no matter how you look at it.

EMAIL "Messages"

✉ INBOX [15/70]

To: Dr. Crane [eaglechristianchurch.com]
Subject: Did Jesus Have Brothers and Sisters?

---Original Message---

You mentioned that the book of James was written by a half-brother of Jesus. I was taught that Jesus did not have any brothers, only cousins.

Reply:

The Bible tells us that Jesus had four brothers: James, Joseph, Simon, and Judas (Matthew 13:55; cf. Acts 1:14; Galatians 1:19). Two of these brothers wrote books of our New Testament: James and Jude. We also know that Jesus had sisters, but no names are given. We know there was more than one sister, because the Bible says "sisters" (Matthew 13:56). These siblings could rightfully be called half-brothers and sisters because while Jesus was the son of Mary, he was conceived by the Holy Spirit. Jesus' siblings were children of Mary and Joseph.

Some Catholics try to deny this teaching by claiming that the words "brother" and "sister" should be translated "cousin." While it is true that the word "brother" can have a broader sense (we are all brothers in Christ), this use is not the natural reading of these passages. One should consider, not only that there is a word for "cousin" in Greek, but it seems more than a little strange to suggest that these "cousins" are so often described as being with Mary the mother of Jesus. There is no reason to believe that these brothers and sisters were anything less than the literal half-brothers and sisters of Jesus.

A second Catholic argument suggests that these "brothers and sisters" were the children of Joseph from a previous marriage. They put forward a theory that Joseph was much older than Mary, was previously married, and when widowed was left with six children—all prior to his betrothal to Mary. This theory has absolutely no basis in fact. If this were true, one would wonder why nothing was mentioned in Scripture. Would this not come up during the engagement? Why would children not be mentioned in Mary and Joseph's trip to Bethlehem (Luke 2:4–7)? Or their trip to Egypt (Matthew 2:13–15)? Or at least on their trip back to Nazareth (Matthew 2:20–23)?

Those who try to explain away Jesus' siblings do so, not from a reading of Scripture, but from an unbiblical belief in a false doctrine called the perpetual virginity of Mary.

EMAIL "Messages"

✉ INBOX [16/70]

To: Dr. Crane [eaglechristianchurch.com]
Subject: Is the Shroud of Turin Authentic?

---Original Message---

I was watching a documentary about the Shroud of Turin on cable TV. What do you think? Is it possible that this really was the burial cloth of Jesus?

Reply:

The "Shroud" is a linen cloth that many claim to be the burial cloth of Jesus (Matthew 27:59; Mark 15:46; Luke 23:53; John 19:40). The Shroud was "discovered" (or at least made public) in the fourteenth century. It is called the Shroud of Turin because of the city that it was kept in—Turin, Italy.

There is much debate on the authenticity of the Shroud of Turin. Some are convinced that it is the burial cloth of Jesus. Others believe it to be a fabrication or even a work of art. There have been dating tests completed that date the Shroud to the tenth century A.D. or later—making it much too late to be that of Christ. Other tests have found spores and pollens that are common to Israel and have been dated to the first century. But none of these tests are conclusive.

This being the case, it is impossible to determine whether or not this is the authentic burial cloth of Christ, nor can it be used as a conclusive proof for the resurrection of Christ.

EMAIL "Messages"

✉ INBOX [17/70]

To: Dr. Crane [eaglechristianchurch.com]
Subject: Is Jesus Currently Alone in Heaven with God?

---Original Message---

I was searching for John 3:16 when I came across John 3:13. It troubled me greatly. I thought that people went to heaven when they died. Is Jesus suggesting that we just rest in our graves until Christ's second coming?

Reply:

At first glance this passage does indeed seem troubling. Jesus clearly says that "No one has ever gone into heaven except the one who came from heaven" (John 3:13). However, the Old Testament says that Elijah "went up to heaven in a whirlwind" (2 Kings 2:11) and that Enoch "walked with God; then he was no more, because God took him away" (Genesis 5:24). Most scholars agree that Enoch was taken to heaven.

We read in John's heavenly visions about the martyrs who cry out "How long, Sovereign Lord . . . until you . . . avenge our blood" (Revelation 6:10)—they seem to have access to the throne of God. Paul tells of his encounter with the "third heaven" which he experienced either bodily or out of body (2 Corinthians 12:2). Even Jesus tells the thief on the cross, "I tell you the truth, today you will be with me in paradise" (Luke 23:43). All these references (and others, cf. Hebrews 11–12) seem to indicate that many people have indeed ascended into heaven. How then do we reconcile these passages?

I believe the key to understanding John 3:13, is to remember that Jesus is setting forth his position of authority and knowledge. Jesus is saying in effect, "No other person can speak from firsthand knowledge about these things like I can." He is not claiming that no one has ascended to heaven, but that no one has ascended to heaven to bring down the message that he brought. Stated another way, he is not denying that anyone else is *in* heaven, but that no one on earth has gone to heaven and *returned* with the message that he is bringing them.

Of course we dare not forget the message Jesus brought from heaven: "For God so loved the world that he gave his one and only Son, that whoever believes in him shall not perish but have eternal life" (John 3:16).

Section Three

Questions about the Bible

EMAIL "Messages"

✉ INBOX [18/70]

To: Dr. Crane [eaglechristianchurch.com]
Subject: What Is the Bible?

---Original Message---

I was in your church Sunday for the first time and I enjoyed your talk. You spoke from a book called "James." After services, I talked with you and asked where I could find this book so I could read it. You told me that it was one of the books in the New Testament of our Bible. I must admit, your response confused me. I thought the Bible was a book. Maybe you can tell me what the Bible is. I was also confused when you talked about Greek words. Why is that important?

Reply:

Thank you for asking this important question. In church, we often wrongly assume that people are familiar with the intricate details of the Bible and we don't explain ourselves as we should. Let me give a brief description of the Bible and how it is organized. Forgive me if I am too detailed—I've actually been writing an entire book on this subject.

To start with, I would posit that the Bible is the collection of God's inspired written word (2 Timothy 3:16–17; 2 Peter 1:20–12). It was written by human authors, who used their knowledge, research, and vocabulary in writing, but it was accomplished under the supernatural guidance of God (God's Holy Spirit), who guided and guarded what they wrote. I believe the Bible is the authoritative rule of faith and practice for Christians and the Church. It serves in many ways as our constitution, play book, our operator's manual.

The Bible, although considered one book, actually consists of two parts, which Christians refer to as the "Old Testament" (O.T.) and the "New Testament" (N.T.). Both of these two large sections also contain individual books—sixty-six in all (thirty-nine in the O.T. and twenty-seven in the N.T.). These individual books were written by various people, at various times (all under God's direction) for various purposes, but all with a common theme—God's redemptive acts in history.

The individual Bible books were later also divided into chapters and verses for ease of reference. Therefore we often cite not only a Bible book (i.e., "James"), but also a chapter and individual verse (James 1:16). The information given so far may be enough to answer your question about the books in the Bible, but from our previous conversation, I am inclined to think you want more. Let me get more specific.

The first division of the Bible (the Old Testament) is much longer (nearly three fourths of our Bible), while the New Testament is much shorter (constituting about one fourth). The Old Testament came into existence over a period of more than a thousand years and deals with the history of God's people before the time of Christ; the New Testament within less than one hundred years and deals with Christian history. The division is much like our distinctions of B.C. and A.D.

The word "testament" is a translation of the word which also means "covenant" or even "agreement." Therefore, when we called one part of our Bible "old" and one part "new," we are making some type of claim—a claim itself which needs to be explained. The Old Testament or Old Covenant prepared the way for Jesus, not only setting a particular people apart from whom the ancestry of Jesus could be traced (the nation of Israel), but also by clearly demarcating important doctrinal issues regarding sin, sacrifice, and the nature of a Holy God. Under much of the Old Covenant (the time before Christ), people were bound by the Mosaic Law and worshiped God in a Temple. The New Covenant (Testament), is the fulfillment of the Old Covenant where Jesus Christ becomes our sacrifice, God's people become the new temple, and Christ becomes the center of our worship.

The thirty-nine books we call the Old Testament can themselves be grouped into four sections. The first five books (Genesis, Exodus, Leviticus, Numbers, and Deuteronomy) are known as the "Torah" (Law) and are ascribed to Moses. The next section includes books we often think of as historical books (Joshua, Judges, Ruth, 1–2 Samuel, 1–2 Kings, 1–2 Chronicles, Ezra, Nehemiah and Esther) and give us the history of the nation of Israel (sometimes, books within this section have been compiled together). The books of poetry include Job, Psalms, Proverbs, Ecclesiastes, and the Song of Solomon. Finally, we have the "Prophets," which are sometimes subdivided into categories called major and minor prophets: Isaiah, Jeremiah, Lamentations, Ezekiel, Daniel, Hosea, Joel, Amos, Obadiah, Jonah, Micah, Nahum, Habakkuk, Zephaniah, Haggai, Zechariah, and Malachi.

These thirty-nine books became fixed into an official list of sacred books which are used by Jewish people. The Greek word for such an official list is "canon." Most of these books were written in Hebrew, which is why the Old Testament is sometimes referred to as the "Hebrew Bible" or the "Jewish Bible." Parts of Daniel and Ezra, plus one verse in Jeremiah and two words in Genesis (a proper name), are written in Aramaic (a sister language to Hebrew).

About two hundred years before Christ, all these books were translated into Greek for the benefit of the increasing number of Jews for whom Greek was the primary language. The Greek Bible, called the "Septuagint" (from the Latin for "seventy"—because of stories about seventy translators) was the Bible used by early Christians, including Jesus and the disciples.

The twenty-seven books of the New Testament tell the story of Jesus and the church. They were all written within sixty years of the death of Jesus—in other words, before the end of the first century. Some of these books (the letters of Paul for example) date from the late forties and fifties. Some may date as late as A.D. 90-95 (the writings of John). The New Testament contains the Gospels (Matthew, Mark, Luke, John) which tell about the ministry of Jesus; a book of the history of the establishment of the church (The Acts of the Apostles); Epistles or letters written to churches or individuals within the church (Romans, 1-2 Corinthians, Galatians, Ephesians, Philippians, Colossians, 1-2 Thessalonians, 1-2 Timothy, Titus, Philemon, Hebrews, James, 1-2 Peter, 1-2-3 John, and Jude); and a book of Prophecy (Revelation).

The New Testament was primarily written in Greek, but also contains a few sayings written in Aramaic.

But the Bible is far more than just a compilation of writings of long ago. The Bible is God revealing himself to man and calling people to himself. It is given to teach us, for rebuking, for correction, and for training in righteousness, so that we can be thoroughly equipped for every good work (2 Timothy 3:16-17). The Bible is God's love letter to mankind. It tells us all that we need to know about life and godliness.

In other words, the Bible isn't simply to be a reference work where we can look things up to make sure we get things right, it is God's word which is meant to equip God's people to become what God designed them to be. It is the manual by which we are to make repairs, refuel, and gain direction. It is a roadmap for life.

For further reading: *How We Got the Bible*, by Neil R. Lightfoot. *The Authority of the Bible*, by Jack Cottrell.

EMAIL "Messages"

✉ INBOX [19/70]

To: Dr. Crane [eaglechristianchurch.com]
Subject: Can You Give Me the Message of the Bible in a Nutshell?

---Original Message---

I am confused about exactly what the Bible is about. Can I ask how you would summarize the message of the Bible in a few words?

Reply:

You should know that I can do very little with only a few words, but I will try. Here is the Bible in a nutshell.

There is one true God who created everything that exists. The focal point of his creation was man (mankind) whom he made in his image. Originally, man had fellowship with God, but he rebelled against God's will and purpose. Sin separated man from God and consequently all of creation was thrown into turmoil. But God loved man so much, he invoked his plan of redemption.

God chose Abraham and his ancestors to serve as a community of God's people. Although they did not live up to God's standards, God's faithfulness to them through many generations served to demonstrate God's justice, mercy, and love, and providentially provided the lineage through whom he would usher in a promised Messiah and Savior. This unique relationship with the nation of Israel provided the opportunity for God to illustrate the cost and consequence of sin and to demonstrate the need for sacrifice.

Then, about 2,000 years ago, God sent his only Son, born of a virgin, to usher in the coming Kingdom of God (a kingdom that is both now, and not yet). The religious establishment rejected Jesus and his claims, and convinced the Romans to kill him by crucifying him on the cross. Jesus died and was buried, but three days later, God raised Jesus physically from the dead. For forty days, Jesus remained with the disciples and then ascended into heaven—with the promise that he would one day return in person and with power to raise the dead and to judge the world. He also promised that he would leave his Spirit (the Holy Spirit) with his followers until he returned. Jesus commissioned the disciples to spread the news and gather in community with each other.

Jesus' death serves as the payment for man's sin. Whoever accepts Jesus and faithfully follows him as Lord and Savior will receive forgiveness and eternal life. These people, as they believe, repent, are baptized, and live as faithful followers of Christ—are trying to live up to what God has already pronounced them to be. Because of this, Christians worship together, encourage one another, and strive to love each other as they live out their faith.

One day, Jesus will return and all evil will be destroyed and there will be a new heaven and a new earth—a reality which will exist without sin or any of sin's results. God's people will be with Jesus and see God face to face, and we will enjoy his presence (and the presence of other believers) forever.

See: *How to Read the Bible Book by Book*, by Gordon Fee and Douglas Stuart; *What the Bible Is All About*, by Henrietta Mears.

EMAIL "Messages"

✉ INBOX [20/70]

To: Dr. Crane [eaglechristianchurch.com]
Subject: Is the Bible to Be Taken Literally or Figuratively?

---Original Message---

I appreciate your faithfulness in preaching the Bible. But I am curious—do you take the Bible to be literal or figurative?

Reply:

Without meaning to sound sarcastic, the answer to your question is, "Yes." No serious student of the Bible would deny that the Bible uses symbols and metaphors at times, while in other instances it describes and depicts real events that happened (or are happening) in the real world.

When Jesus says, for example, in the Gospel of John, "I am the living bread" (6:51), or "I am the gate" (10:9), or "I am the vine" (15:5); are we to literally picture Jesus as a loaf, a gate, or a vine? Of course not. Or we might think of a great prophetic passage from the book of Daniel 7. The passage speaks of Daniel having a dream in which four "beasts" come up out of the sea: a lion with eagle's wings, a bear with three ribs in its mouth, a leopard with four wings, and a monster with ten horns. All of these beasts are obviously to be taken metaphorically. No one needs ask if these animals actually existed at some point in time, and it would be foolish to demand to go see them in a zoo or a museum. And yet, these metaphorical images represented a concrete reality. These animals represented the kingdoms of Babylon, Medo-Persia, Greece, and Rome.

The Bible also contains accounts which are to be taken quite literally. Much of the Bible is recorded history—actual events that happened at a certain place at a certain time. I believe the birth of Jesus, his life and ministry, his miracles, his death, his burial, his resurrection, his ascension—were all actual, literal, and physical events. I believe this to be true of Christ's future second coming as well.

Simply put, some of the Bible is prose and poetry—it should be understood as prose and poetry. Some of the Bible contains hyperbole and metaphor—it should be understood as hyperbole and metaphor. Much of the Bible is historical narrative—it should be understood as historical narrative. The same could be said of all the other various literary forms we might find within the Bible's cover, whether it be prophecy, hymn, didactic, or doxology.

It is not a matter of interpreting the Bible literally or figuratively. Instead, it is a matter of interpreting the Bible naturally in light of the genre of each book and each section of writing.

The interpretation of the Bible is a huge and wonderful task. We must do so with careful and prayerful study, remembering that the Bible is indeed God's gift to us. We should do our best to correctly handle the word of truth (2 Timothy 2:15).

EMAIL "Messages"

✉ INBOX [21/70]

To: Dr. Crane [eaglechristianchurch.com]
Subject: What Evidence Do You Have That the Bible Is Accurate?

---Original Message---

I appreciate the fact that you consistently preach the Bible. But what evidence do you have that the Bible is true and accurate?

Reply:

I'd like to answer this question by using an acrostic—M.A.P.S. The Bible is unlike any other work of ancient history (or, for that matter, any other religious book) in the evidence of its authenticity and accuracy.

> M. The Bible has unparalleled MANUSCRIPT evidence. Because of time and wear, many of the historical documents from the ancient world have few manuscripts to which we can refer. This is especially true when one considers the secular historians and philosophers. For instance, we only have eight copies of the historical work of Herodotus, five copies of Aristotle's writings, and seven copies from the historian Pliny.
>
> When we consider the New Testament, however, we find a completely different scenario. We have today in our possession 5,300 Greek manuscripts, another 10,000 Latin Vulgates, and 9,300 manuscripts of other varieties (Armenian, Coptic, Ethiopic, Georgian, Nubian)—giving us more than 24,000 partial or complete manuscript copies in existence today. I have not even mentioned lectionaries or writings of early church fathers (Clement, Ignatius, Polycarp, etc.). We have

such a wealth of manuscripts we can be assured of the Bible's accuracy.

A. The Bible has been proven to be historically reliable by numerous ARCHAEOLOGICAL discoveries. The spade is the friend of the Bible. To date, more than 25,000 archaeological discoveries have verified the names of persons, places, events, and customs mentioned in the Bible. Open a page of the Bible and you will discover that it mentions real cities, real places, real events. You can visit the mountains, lakes, and rivers it describes.

P. The Bible, unlike any other religious book, has demonstrated itself to be the word of God through its ability to predict the future. There are literally hundreds of very specific PROPHECIES in the Bible that were fulfilled hundreds and even thousands of years after they were spoken. No other religious book can verify itself in this way.

S. Finally, the Bible's accuracy, predictive nature, and archaeological evidence are so amazing that it cannot be STATISTICALLY explained in any other way. Let me give you just a couple of examples. What is the statistically probability that twelve men would all die for a known lie—and yet the Apostles are all martyred (John was banished to the island of Patmos) after having been given the opportunity to deny their faith? What is the statistical probability that a book which is actually a collection of 66 different books written down by more than 40 different authors over a period of more than 1500 years on three different continents and in three different languages can contain one central message and have one united theme? The Bible addresses life's most controversial topics from beginning to end and yet miraculously remains absolutely consistent and internally harmonious from beginning to end.

These evidences MAP out the course for us and give us a compelling case for the divine origin and the historical reliability of the Bible.

For further information, you can listen to Dr. Crane's "M.A.P.S." sermon at www.eaglechristianchurch.com.

EMAIL "Messages"

✉ INBOX [22/70]

To: Dr. Crane [eaglechristianchurch.com]
Subject: Has the Bible Been Corrupted?

---Original Message---

Hasn't the Bible been corrupted as it was translated hundreds of times down through the centuries?

Reply:

The Bible has been translated hundreds of times into hundreds of different languages down through the centuries. But this process of translation has actually served to prove the remarkable accuracy of the Bible. Let me give you several examples.

First, when it comes to the New Testament, we have literally thousands of partial and complete handwritten manuscripts, written in the original language (Greek), some of which date back within one or two hundred years from when they were originally written. These manuscripts allow scholars to verify that the Bible we have today is the same Bible as the early church had.

Second, we have all the writings of the church fathers (commentaries, sermons, lectures, and letters from early leaders of the church) in which these men quote the New Testament over 86,000 times. From their quotations alone, scholars are able to reconstruct more than 99 percent of the New Testament (there are only 11 verses in the New Testament for which we do not have a citation from an early church father).

Third, all the many translations we have of Scripture show the remarkable consistency in which the Bible has been translated.

Early Coptic, Syrian, and Aramaic translations are of particular importance.

These evidences verify conclusively that the original text of the Bible has been accurately preserved.

EMAIL "Messages"

✉ INBOX [23/70]

To: Dr. Crane [eaglechristianchurch.com]
Subject: Is the King James Version the Only Authorized Version?

---Original Message---

Is the "King James Version" the only authorized version of Scripture?

Reply:

A strong movement of Christians today is known as "King James-Only" Christians. As a rule, they believe that the King James Version (KJV) is the only reliable text and that all other Bible translations are at best, inferior, and at worst, harmful. They refer to the KJV as "the Authorized Version."[1] Their exact beliefs vary: 1) some King James-Only adherents argue that God had the KJV written so that, through the translators, he could produce a perfect English Bible—they hold that the KJV is inspired in its translation. 2) Others argue only that the text from which the KJV was translated is inspired. This text is called the *Textus Receptus*,[2] and only translations that rely specifically on this Greek text are acceptable—primarily the KJV. 3) A few suggest that the *Textus Receptus* is merely the best of the manuscripts available and therefore should

---

1. Actually, the KJV was never "authorized" by King, Parliament, or church council. It was set in motion by King James and was, at the time, a great step forward.

2. The *Textus Receptus* was a good beginning work in gathering the known old texts, but its faults were that it missed the many later finds, most of which dated much earlier. Modern computerization has helped catalog the variant readings and purify the text itself. Scholars today use *The American Bible Society Greek Text*.

be used in translation—which again basically limits the playing field to the KJV.

Most Christians who hold these views come from a fundamental Baptist position, although Mormons (the Church of Jesus Christ of Latter-day Saints) would concur. Sadly, the King James-Only controversy is an issue based on inaccurate arguments. It centers around a couple of basic issues, which are as follows.

A. Proper Manuscript Theory. This comes into play with what are known as "variances" in Greek texts. When a translator comes across a variant reading, how should it be translated? When evaluating the "families" of manuscripts, one must decide whether they will follow a "multiple manuscript theory" or a "closest to the source theory." Simply put, should a translator choose from a larger group of late manuscripts, or rely on the smaller group of more ancient manuscripts that is now available? The KJV chooses to follow the multiple manuscript theory, while all other modern translations tend to rely on the more ancient texts.

B. Modern Vocabulary. The second issue concerns producing a translation that uses a good, modern vocabulary. The purpose of a translation is to accurately bring the meaning of Hebrew, Aramaic, and Greek words into a modern, understandable language. The question that needs to be asked is: "What words most accurately reflect to a contemporary audience the intended meaning of a passage of Scripture to aid their understanding?" Specifically, are the words of "King James English" more precise, accurate, or understandable, than modern language versions to a modern audience?

Let me briefly answer the three views given previously (1–3):

VIEW #1. The King James Version is itself inspired.
To really understand the issue, you must understand the background of the KJV. The KJV was actually an attempt to put the

Bible into the modern vernacular of the time (see "B" above). The KJV was first published in 1611. Few realize that the KJV itself has had multiple revisions: 1611,[3] 1612, 1613, 1616, 1629, 1638, 1650,[4] 1660, 1683, 1727, 1762, 1769, 1873, and 1888. Each of these twenty versions differ in translation.[5]

The KJV Bible used today (1888) is based primarily on a major revision, not of the 1873 version, but a revamping of the 1769 version. This current edition came 277 years after the first edition of 1611. If the 1611 edition is the true Word of God (as many claim) why is it no longer in use? And if it is not the 1611 version, which one is "God's perfect word?" Why is the 1888 version a reworking of the 1769? Why not rework the 1873 edition? And so forth.

VIEWS #2 and #3. Only versions (translations) based on the *Textus Receptus* are valid, because it is the inspired text (or at least the most accurate text).

A brief history is in order. Jerome was responsible for translating the Bible into "New" Latin in the late fourth century (A.D. 383–405). He wanted to put the Bible in the common vernacular rather than using the "Old" Latin text the church was using. Interestingly enough, he was criticized for his efforts of translating a new Bible—people thought the Old Latin was the most appropriate translation. Jerome had the disadvantage of not having a complete Greek text. Where Jerome had Greek texts, he translated them into New Latin. At points where no Greek texts were available, he translated the Old Latin into a Greek text, and then proceeded to translate his new Greek text into New Latin. Despite its shortcomings, Jerome produced a remarkable text in the *Latin Vulgate*. His translation, with its limitations, became the Bible of the Church for a thousand years.

---

3. There are two different versions of the 1611 version.

4. There are six different versions of the 1650 edition.

5. This does not include the New King James Version, which most King James-Only adherents also reject.

In 1516, Catholic scholar Desiderius Erasmus translated a text from Greek (based on the Greek text of the *Latin Vulgate*—Jerome's Greek text). Erasmus took less than a year to produce his text. Because of the speed of his work, two scholars (Robert Stephanus and Theodore Beza) later revised his text to correct obvious errors in his translation. The works of these three men combined, came to be known as *Complutesian Polyglot*. This manuscript was the translation used to produce the first edition of the King James Bible in 1611.

It was not until 1624 that the Elzevir brothers (Abraham and Bonaventure) initially published their own text which they later revised in 1633. The preface of this second version (1633) claimed that this text was "the best received of all." This "received text" became known as the *Textus Receptus* (based on their claim in the preface). This text, however, has undergone significant changes producing over 30 different editions. It is, however, the *Textus Receptus* which is behind the subsequent versions of the KJV. All differ from the Erasmus text, and the Jerome text (as well as other versions of the *Textus Receptus*) in more than a hundred instances. This brings up the issue of "variances." What do you do when a particular verse has different manuscript evidence (even within the same family of manuscripts)? This solution supplied by the translators of the KJV was the "multiple manuscript theory"—when there are variants—count the number of manuscripts to determine which "reading" to use. Of course at the time of translation, Jerome's *Latin Vulgate* outnumbered all others and many of the most significant manuscript finds were yet to be discovered: the Dead Sea Scrolls, the *Codex Vaticanus*, the *Codex Sinaiticus*, the *Bodmer II Texts*, the *Chester Beatty Papyri*, the *John Rolands Text*, etc.

The problem: Most King James adherents believe that either the KJV or the *Textus Receptus* are inspired. The difficulty with such a view is that both have undergone major editing in the past and still contain inadequacies. This leaves only two options: either the KJV or *Textus Receptus* is wrong, or God has inspired errors in His word.

Conclusion.

In view of this history, I need to make a couple of remarks. First, after all is said and done, the KJV is remarkably accurate. I would be happy to use this version if it were the only one that was available. Today, however, literal translations like the New American Standard Version and the New International Version (and others) are much more accurate and more readable, which greatly enhances the average Christian's understanding. Dynamic translations have also been produced which accurately reflect the intended meaning of Scripture (God's Word or The New Living Translation, and others).

Second, we should remember that the KJV itself was an attempt to put the Bible in the hands of the common man in the language of the time. It served the same purpose as do our modern translations.

Third, the KJV, while remarkably accurate, does not reflect the best ancient Greek texts that are now available; it is based on a faulty translation theory (multiple manuscript theory) and it does not communicate in the language of the common person today.

Fourth, most who hold to a King James-Only position are not themselves Greek or Hebrew scholars. Those who argue *King James Only* actually prefer the King James Version of the Bible *above the Greek texts* themselves. They are typically untrained and have not studied either Greek, Hebrew, or the subject of Bible translation.[6]

---

6. This is also true of those who write these types of books on a popular level.

Finally, those who hold to a King James-Only tradition, although their views are widespread and available in print,[7] do not understand the real issues at hand, nor is their conclusion defensible.

For further reading: *A History of the English Bible*, by Jonathan Underwood. *Selecting a Translation of the Bible*, by Lewis Foster.

---

7. Show me the scholarly work written by a Greek scholar (not written on merely a popular level) that argues in favor of the King James-Only controversy. I am not aware of any that would hold this view. I am aware of a multitude of books, written from both a popular and technical level, by scholars debunking this view. Let me name a couple of good books on biblical manuscripts and translations from notable sources: *A General Introduction to the Bible* by Geisler and Nix; *General Biblical Introduction* by Miller; *Taking a Stand for the Bible* by Ankerberg/Burroughs; *The Canon of Scripture* by F.F. Bruce; *The Search for the Original Bible* by Price; *The Origin of the Bible* by Comfort; *How We Got the Bible* by Lightfoot; *The Authority of the Bible* by Miller; *The History of the English Bible* by Underwood; *Seeking a Translation of the Bible* by Foster; etc.

EMAIL "Messages"

✉ INBOX [24/70]

To: Dr. Crane [eaglechristianchurch.com]
Subject: What Bible Translation Should I Use?

---Original Message---

I am a new Christian and want to get a nice Bible, but when I walked into the Bible bookstore there was a whole wall of different kinds of Bibles. What Bible translation should I get?

Reply:

The key to answering your question is the acknowledgment that our English Bibles are indeed translations—the New Testament being originally written in Greek and the Old Testament being originally written in Hebrew (with a smattering of Aramaic in both Old and New). Anyone who has endeavored to translate a foreign language realizes the difficulty of the task.

Let me mention just two of these difficulties. First, it is often difficult to consistently find a word-for-word equivalent when moving from one language to another. It is often necessary to use a phrase (several words) to depict a certain word (or vice versa). Even if there is a "precise" word equivalent, the precision of a word might cause a sentence to be difficult to understand (the English words "propitiation," "justification," and "reconciliation" would serve as good examples).

A second difficulty arises out of the fact that word order is not consistent from one language to another. The question arises, how closely does a translation need to stay to the original order to be true to the biblical text? Translators must work through these and other issues when translating a particular passage.

In dealing with these translation difficulties, there are two primary schools of thought. One has as its goal to produce a literal word-for-word translation. While being true to the text, this translation can suffer from not only being difficult to understand, but awkward, cumbersome, and stale. A second goal is to create a thought-for-thought translation. Often called "dynamic translations," these Bibles attempt to free-up the text, but in so doing, some liberties and license are taken.

This being said, most all of the modern-day translations do a remarkable job of putting the Word of God into our modern vernacular. Two very good "word-for-word" translations are the "New American Standard Bible" (NASB) and more recently, the "English Standard Version" (ESV). In most instances, one could cheat on their New Testament Greek test by using one of these versions. These make very good study Bibles, but do suffer from being more difficult to read (especially out loud).

I would also recommend two very good "dynamic" translations. One is simply called "God's Word." The other is the "New Living Translation" (NLT). Both do an excellent job of giving biblical explanations for difficult concepts. They are accurate thought-by-thought Bibles that are easy to read and understand.

When I preach, I currently use the "New International Version" (NIV). It is not necessarily my favorite, but it is easy to read from the pulpit, tries to balance a word-for-word translation with readability, and is currently the most widely read Bible. The NIV has undergone a new revision in 2011.

Before closing, I need to define one other term. There is a difference between a translation (either word-for-word or thought-for-thought) and a paraphrase. A paraphrase is not a translation, but simply a person's thoughts about what they think they have read in their Bible. These can be very helpful and enjoyable to read, but they should never be substituted for a true translation or used for serious biblical study. The most famous "paraphrase" of yesteryear is "The Living Bible." More recently, Eugene Peterson's, "The Message," has become very popular. These can be used for supplemental reading, but should not be used as your primary Bible.

In my Bible reading I enjoy reading from several different Bible versions and even an occasional paraphrase. The important thing is to make Bible reading part of your regular discipleship process. I would recommend you get a "good" (even expensive) Bible and make it a priority to read it. Make it one of your life's treasures.

EMAIL "Messages"

✉ INBOX [25/70]

To: Dr. Crane [eaglechristianchurch.com]
Subject: What about the Gospel of Thomas?

---Original Message---

What about the Gospel of Thomas? I have read that it should be included among our Bible books.

Reply:

There has been a recent influx of books, both scholarly and on the popular level, that are claiming that the Gospels were only four among many other similar works that were around in the early church. Some of those making these claims actually assert that Matthew, Mark, Luke, and John are inferior to other works which were discarded, suppressed, and even banned by the church.

While it is true that other documents have turned up over time, none of them bear the stamp of authenticity of our Gospels, none are on the same plane as Scripture, none fall within the continuity of Scripture (they don't seem to fit), and none of these other writings date to an acceptable period of time within the lifetime of the Apostles of Jesus.

The best known, and one of the longest of these writings is a book known as the Gospel of Thomas to which your question refers. It is part of a larger collection called the *Nag Hammadi Texts* which were found in Upper Egypt in 1945. The Gospel of Thomas is written in Coptic (a language spoken in Egypt), but is said to be a translation from the Syriac language (a language quite like the Aramaic that Jesus spoke). If this is true (it remains speculation), the document can be placed fairly early. The problem, however, is that the Syriac language (while being similar to Aramaic and arriving early), dates not to the first century, but to the end of the second century (over a hundred years after the four Canonical Gospels were written and certainly seventy years after they were in widespread use). Furthermore, despite efforts to prove these documents authentic, they represent a world-view known as "Gnosticism" (the belief in a special knowledge of hidden truth) which highlights the fact that these were "counterfeit" writings.

It is only pseudo-theologians, with their footing on very shaky ground, who would suggest that these writings represent early Christianity and should be included among the writings we would call Scripture.

EMAIL "Messages"

✉ INBOX [26/70]

To: Dr. Crane [eaglechristianchurch.com]
Subject: What about Apocryphal Books?

---Original Message---

Why do some Bibles have more books in them than others? The idea that something might be missing from my Bible is quite troubling to me.

Reply:

Today there is very little discussion concerning which of our Bible books rightfully belong in the Bible. That being said, it is interesting to find that the Catholic Bible and the Bible used by most Protestants are different. While both Bibles have twenty-seven books in the New Testament, the Catholic Bible has several additional books. These extra books are generally referred to as the "Apocrypha" (meaning hidden). The Roman Catholic Church refers to these additional books as "deuterocanonical" (second canon), acknowledging that these were not part of the original canon, but accepted later. The Catholic Church also acknowledges that these books are not Scripture in the same sense as other Old Testament books—calling them valuable, but less than scriptural in authority. Many scholars appreciate the history of these books (especially 1 Maccabees and Ecclesiasticus) because they help reveal the development of Israel between the writing of Malachi and Matthew.

The Old Testament Apocrypha includes either fourteen or fifteen (depending on your method of counting) books that were written between 300 B.C. and A.D. 100. Three of these fifteen books are not considered canonical by the Roman Catholic Church. In Catholic Bibles, the remaining twelve are interspersed among and attached to the other books of the Old Testament.

There are many reasons why these books are rejected as Scripture. Let me give you five. 1) They were never included in the Hebrew canon of the Old Testament. 2) They were never accepted as canonical by Jesus and his apostles (New Testament writers quote from nearly every O.T. book, but never from any of the Apocrypha). 3) They were never accepted as Scripture by Jewish or Christian writers of the first century. 4) They do not bear the intrinsic qualities of inspiration (great portions of these books are obviously fictional, contain historical, grammatical, chronological, and geographical errors). 5) They have always been shrouded with uncertainty and have always been acknowledged as inferior.

The apocryphal books, therefore, are rightfully rejected from our Bibles.

EMAIL "Messages"

✉ INBOX [27/70]

To: Dr. Crane [eaglechristianchurch.com]
Subject: What is the Jesus Seminar?

---Original Message---

I keep hearing about the "Jesus Seminar" and the attempt to discover the historical Jesus. Isn't the Jesus recorded for us in the Bible historical?

Reply:

The "Jesus Seminar" is the brainchild of a "scholar" by the name of Robert Funk. Funk believes that the "true Jesus" has been hidden by Christian traditions, myths, and legends that the church has "developed" over a period of 2000 years. Funk and his cronies (a group comprised almost entirely of people who deny the inspiration, authority, and inerrancy of the Bible) peel away Scripture in an attempt to discover who Jesus truly was and what he truly said. The problem is that their main agenda is not to discover "Jesus," but to attack what the Bible clearly says about Jesus and discredit his message.

The "Jesus Seminar" divides Jesus' words into various categories to which they assign colored beads based on how accurate they feel the Bible's words to be. They literally "vote" on each verse recorded in the Gospel as to its authenticity. Words assigned a red bead are attributed to Jesus. Words given pink beads represent words Jesus might possibly have said. Words marked by a grey bead indicate words they think highly improbable. Words assigned beads of black represent words (in their opinion) Jesus definitely did not say. It is telling that black beads outnumber the red, pink and grey beads combined. Only a few verses in all of the Gospels are deemed authentic.

For instance, nearly the entire Gospel of John receives a black bead—virtually none of it is considered by them to be representative of Christ. They prefer a counterfeit work called "the Gospel of Thomas" which receives both pink and red beads (see the question regarding the Gospel of Thomas).

Far from being a scholastic attempt to understand the historical Jesus, this "seminar" is an offensive farce. Are we really to believe that a group of "scholars" today can more accurately determine what Jesus did and did not say (by casting votes) than the authors of the Gospels who wrote in the same century in which Jesus lived and taught?

The so-called "scholars" do not believe in the deity of Christ, miracles, or the resurrection—primarily because they do not believe Scripture. The true purpose of the "Jesus Seminar" is not to find the "historical Jesus," but to undermine the word of God, enabling them paint a picture of a Jesus of their own making.

EMAIL "Messages"

✉ INBOX [28/70]

To: Dr. Crane [eaglechristianchurch.com]
Subject: Shouldn't We Expect More Bible?

---Original Message---

If God revealed himself to people in the past, isn't it possible that God would continue to reveal himself to people in the future? That being the case, shouldn't we expect more of the Bible to be written and compiled?

Reply:

There is no reason to believe that God should add to his Word, and every reason to believe that he won't. The Bible begins with the very beginning of humanity—Genesis; and ends with the culmination of history as we know it—Revelation. The pages in between give us everything that is needed for life and godliness. Paul says, "All Scripture is God-breathed and is useful for teaching, rebuking, correcting and training in righteousness, so that the man of God may be thoroughly equipped for every good work" (2 Timothy 3:16).

If further books are needed, logically that would mean that our current Bible is incomplete—that it doesn't tell us everything we need to know. That would contradict what the Bible says about itself.

Although it only applies directly to the book of Revelation, Revelation teaches us about adding to God's Word: "I warn everyone who hears the words of the prophecy of this book: If anyone adds anything to them, God will add to him the plagues described in this book. And if anyone takes words away from this book of prophecy, God will take away from him his share in the tree of life and in the holy city" (22:18–20).

The Bible contains everything we need for salvation and holiness. There is not a single situation in life that cannot be addressed by the use of Scripture. What started in Genesis finds completion in Revelation. Could God add to the Bible? Of course he could. But there is no reason, logically, biblically, or theologically, to believe that he will do so.

Section Four

Questions about Salvation

EMAIL "Messages"

✉ INBOX [29/70]

To: Dr. Crane [eaglechristianchurch.com]
Subject: Can I Be a Christian If I've Got Doubts?

---Original Message---

I want to believe in Jesus. I think I do believe in Jesus, but I still have some doubts. Is it possible to believe in Jesus and still have areas of uncertainty?

Reply:

Everyone (preachers included) experience doubt from time to time. It is helpful to understand that doubting does not have to destroy faith. In fact, doubting just might have the opposite effect. Personally, I believe that the strongest faith is one which has resolved doubts. For Christian faith to be credible faith, it must be an examined faith. If Christianity cannot be defended, it should not be believed! I am a Christian minister precisely because I have wrestled with doubt and have determined Christianity credible. Paul speaks of this when he says, "Test everything, hold on to the good" (1 Thessalonians 5:21).

It might be helpful to explain that doubt and unbelief are not the same. Doubt is not the opposite of faith, nor is it the same as unbelief. Doubt is on the continuum between faith and unbelief. The biblical difference between doubt and unbelief is a crucial difference. Unbelief usually describes a person who does not or will not believe—it is a settled determination against belief. Doubt, on the other hand, wants to believe, and even will believe—if there is sufficient evidence.

I love the story of the man who comes to Jesus seeking healing for his ailing son. He asks Jesus "if" he can do anything. Jesus essentially says, "What do you mean 'if'?" At that point Jesus says, "Everything is possible for him who believes." The man responds, "I do believe, help me overcome my unbelief" (Mark 9:24).

To some extent, faith contains at least a microcosm of doubt. This is not to say that major doubt is not serious. Unanswered doubts can lead a person in the wrong direction—toward disbelief. A person should do whatever they can to resolve doubts in order to make a strong informed decision about Christ.

I hope that helps. I don't doubt it will.

EMAIL "Messages"

✉ INBOX [30/70]

To: Dr. Crane [eaglechristianchurch.com]
Subject: Can You Lose Your Salvation?

---Original Message---

I have heard the doctrine of "Once Saved, Always Saved." Can you lose your salvation?

Reply:

This is certainly a relevant issue and one that needs to be addressed. How a person answers this query, serves for some as a litmus test to determine orthodoxy. And yet, to be honest, I don't like the question. This topic has been hotly debated, dividing the church for hundreds of years, and creating much animosity between Christian brothers who have questioned the salvation and integrity of all who have disagreed with them. Did you notice that I used the language of "Christian brothers"? Although many make it out to be of utmost importance, I don't believe this particular question makes it on to a heavenly entrance exam. How one answers this question neither validates nor invalidates their Christian faith.

The debate is often couched in terms of two individuals: John Calvin, and his hand-picked successor, Jacobus Arminius. While they saw eye to eye on most theological issues, they divided over this one in particular. Calvin answered the above question "no," while Arminius disagreed. The truth of the matter, however, is that the two were not that far apart in their opinions. The apparent dichotomy was actually an issue of semantics (and a small part of a much bigger issue over which the two men disagreed—free will and the sovereignty of God).

But how could two mutually exclusive answers be closer than they appear? Let me briefly explain. The Arminian, while affirming that it is possible to "lose one's salvation," would not suggest that a person is "in" one moment, and "out" of God's favor the next—as if God needed "white-out" in the book of life. The Calvinist, while arguing that when a person is saved, he is "sealed," and God's sealing cannot be undone (2 Corinthians 1:22; Ephesians 1:13)—if they saw a person who claimed to be a Christian and yet was living a life of debauchery, would likely assert the person was never saved in the first place. Both not only qualify their answers, in most instances, the two are standing back to back, looking in opposite directions.

As mentioned before, I actually don't like the question at all. When we speak of "losing" something, it means you formerly had something of value, and for whatever reason, the thing you wanted to possess has disappeared. Look up the word "lose" and you will find this definition: "To become unable to find, to have taken by accident, to fail to keep or maintain."

No one, not even the most stringent Arminian, believes that salvation is something that can be misplaced, taken, or lost by accident. The question that needs to be asked is not whether you can lose your salvation, but whether you can spit in the face of God and walk away. The bigger issue involved is actually a question of free will and the sovereignty of God. Is man capable of choosing to accept or reject God, or does God choose unconditionally?

See: Hebrews 5:11—6:12; James 1:2, 9, 16, 19; 2:1, 5, 14, 15; 3:1, 10, 12; 4:11; 5:7, 9, 10, 12, 19; John 15:1–14.

EMAIL "Messages"

✉ INBOX [31/70]

To: Dr. Crane [eaglechristianchurch.com]
Subject: What Is the Unpardonable Sin?

---Original Message---

What is the unpardonable sin and have I committed it?

Reply:

You are obviously referencing Matthew 12:31–32 (cf. Mark 3:28–30). The situation in these texts involved religious leaders who accused Jesus of performing miracles by the power of Satan, when in truth, Jesus was empowered by the Spirit of God. In so doing, the religious leaders were rejecting the only one who could save them. One cannot be forgiven while they reject the one in whom forgiveness is available.

In Hebrews, the author refers to a similar situation. He speaks of one who rejects Christ after being enlightened, tasting the heavenly gift, sharing in the Holy Spirit, tasting the goodness of the word of God, and the powers of the coming age (Hebrews 6:4–5). These people cannot be brought back to repentance because (while) they are crucifying the Son of God all over again (Hebrews 6:6). These people (because they are in this condition of rejecting Jesus) cannot be forgiven for the same reason that Jesus' enemies in the Gospels could not be forgiven—they have rejected the one in whom forgiveness is available.

To knowingly, continually, and intentionally reject Jesus is unpardonable, because the person who is doing the rejecting cannot look to the person through whom forgiveness and pardon are possible. No sin is beyond God's forgiveness (even rejecting Jesus) as long as the person truly repents and seeks forgiveness through Jesus Christ. But those who continually and terminally reject Jesus will be unpardoned—it is the unpardonable sin.

EMAIL "Messages"

✉ INBOX [32/70]

To: Dr. Crane [eaglechristianchurch.com]
Subject: What about Those Who Have Never Heard the Gospel?

---Original Message---

I am disturbed by your teaching. While I know and believe that all salvation comes from Jesus Christ's death and resurrection, I also believe that it is for all, with no exceptions. I don't think that knowing about Jesus Christ and consciously accepting him is a prerequisite to salvation. If it is, then what is to become of the millions of people who preceded Christ, and the billions after him who have never had the opportunity to know him? While I don't believe that all religions are equally good, I also don't believe that in God's infinite mercy and justice, that all people who don't know Christ will be condemned if they have led good lives in accordance with their beliefs, to the best of their ability. It's not for each of us to judge them. For the record, I have been a Christian for almost 83 years, as are my wife and six kids, although several of them follow other faiths.

Reply:
I am glad to hear of your 83 years as a Christian. I also certainly understand your concern for all the "millions of people who preceded Christ" and "the billions after him who have never had the opportunity to know him." Personally, I am more than content to let God be God and let him decide who will and will not be accepted. God can (and will) do what he desires with those who have not heard the gospel (see Romans 2:6–16). I do know that God is merciful and gracious (Psalms 103:8). He does not want anyone

to perish (2 Peter 3:9). He will judge with righteousness and equity (Psalm 98:9). And he will judge people based on what they know through the testimony of creation and their own conscience (Romans 1:20; 2:12–15). I also know that by this standard, God could righteously condemn all people (Romans 3:10, 23). What he will do, however, is certainly not for me to determine, nor will he ask my opinion.

Still, as a Bible-believing Christian minister, I am guided by his Word. And the only way we can have any semblance of certainty of someone's eternal destiny (according to the Bible) is by what they have done with Jesus Christ. Let me quote John 3:16: "For God so loved the world that he gave his one and only Son, that whoever BELIEVES in him shall not perish, but have eternal life." Those are not my words, and they seem to contain a condition. I could also quote Mark 16:16, "Whoever BELIEVES . . . will be saved, but whoever DOES NOT BELIEVE will be condemned." While these verses do not speak of those who haven't heard the gospel (and therefore had no opportunity to believe), they certainly do speak of those who have heard and not believed.

Which leads me to your statement, "I don't think that knowing about Jesus Christ and consciously accepting him is a prerequisite to salvation . . . While I know and believe that all salvation comes from Jesus Christ's death and resurrection, I also believe that it is for all, with no exceptions." It seems to me that the Bible has spoken directly to this—it is available to those who BELIEVE. Is your personal opinion (that a person need not consciously accept Christ) based on a particular verse in Scripture which says everyone, regardless of their belief will be saved? If so, I need to be made aware of it. For clarification: are all those people who REJECT Christ included in your list of the "saved"? Is heaven universally occupied by all people regardless of what they have done with Christ? Would that demonstrate "God's infinite justice"? While I know people who believe this way—their argument is not with me, but with what is recorded for us in Scripture.

Ultimately, the question is whether or not one believes the Bible to be the Word of God. Certainly a person has every right to accept or reject the Bible as God's Word. My disconnect comes when a person seemingly quotes the Bible at one point, but then does not believe it at another. It seems inconsistent to accept and reject it in the same breath! If you believe Jesus, you must believe Jesus' words: "Small is the gate and narrow the road that leads to life, and only a few find it" (Matthew 7:14), and "I am the way and the truth and the life. No one comes to the Father except through me" (John 14:6).

For further reading: *How Lost are the Heathen?* by J. Oswald Sanders.

EMAIL "Messages"

✉ INBOX [33/70]

To: Dr. Crane [eaglechristianchurch.com]
Subject: What is Universalism?

---Original Message---

I was talking to a friend who said she was a universalist and was trying to convince me to believe the same. I didn't know what "universalism" meant or how to respond to her.

Reply:

Universalism is a belief system that states that all mankind will ultimately be saved—regardless of what they did with Jesus. It is not difficult to see why this particular view of salvation would be popular for some. But the question we must face is not whether we would like to believe it, but whether it is true.

The universalist argues that since God is love, his love must triumph over his wrath, and every human being will one day find himself within the embrace of that love. Universalists cannot bring themselves to believe that millions or billions of people could be estranged from God.

But if universalism is true, it actually destroys the very work of the church and the message of the Bible. The purpose of the preacher would not be to win people to Jesus, but to inform them that they are redeemed. Let me point out just a few of the problems that come with a belief in universalism.

1. Universalism denies any true freedom of the will. If everyone will be saved, then there is no way that anyone can say "no" to

God. Everyone will be saved regardless of whether they want to be saved or not.

2. Universalism denies the authority of the written Word of God. The Bible constantly makes the distinction between good and evil, eternal life and eternal death, light and darkness, the righteous and the wicked, the saved and the lost, the sheep and the goats, the condemned and the forgiven, heaven and hell, etc. The contrasts could not be clearer. In Scripture there is a final and irremediable separation between the saved and the lost (Matthew 7:13; 13:41–42; 25:32–46; 2 Thessalonians 1:8–9; 2 Peter 2:9; Revelation 14:9–11; 20:10–15, etc.). If universalism were true, even Jesus' words are relegated to the insignificant: "But small is the gate and narrow the road that leads to life, and only a few find it" (Matthew 7:14).

3. Universalism minimizes the gravity of sin and the call to holiness. Universalists believe that the seriousness of sin (warned about throughout Scripture) has been highly exaggerated, and that the need to live out our faith has been unnecessarily propped up. Universalism teaches that everyone is saved, and no one is lost—regardless of what they have done and in spite of their relationship (or lack thereof) to Christ. Are we really to believe that the Atheist will receive the same end as the martyred Saint? If all men reach the same end in life—where is the incentive to avoid sensuality and promote holy living?

4. Universalism violates the Bible's teaching on final judgement. If universalism is true, shouldn't it be called final acquittal? Wouldn't acquitting all people actually be a violation of the very sense of justice? Or should we conduct similar funeral services for both Judas and James, Nero and Paul, Martin Luther and Hitler? (See Matthew 25:31–32; 2 Corinthians 5:10; Hebrews 9:27: 2 Peter 2:9; Jude 14–15.)

5. Universalism robs preaching of its urgency. If universalism is true, why the harsh warning in such passages as 2 Corinthians

5:10; Hebrews 4:7; and Hebrews 10:27–29? Contrary to what the universalist might teach, there is need for a renewed emphasis on the teaching of Scripture that all mankind without Christ is lost!

One final thought. If universalism was true—and all are going to heaven regardless of what they believe—why did your friend feel compelled to try to convince you to believe it?

EMAIL "Messages"

✉ INBOX [34/70]

To: Dr. Crane [eaglechristianchurch.com]
Subject: What about Infant Baptism?

---Original Message---

Do passages about household baptism in the Bible teach infant baptism?

Reply:

I appreciate your faithfulness in determining the truth of God's word and seeking answers! Keep questioning, it's healthy! The accounts of household baptisms (primarily in the book of Acts) are often used in support of infant baptism. I am leery of these arguments for several reasons.

First, to conclude that a mention of a "household" must include infants is an argument from silence. The mention of a household does not describe the ages of the participants in any way with the exception of the presence of an adult. In fact, take a survey of the majority of households at any given time and you will likely not find an infant. The fact is, a mention of the word "household" is neutral—it neither requires nor prohibits the presence of an infant. Actually, it doesn't require children of any age.

Second, there are only four references in the New Testament concerning household baptisms and, if anything, they contain something that would actually *exclude* infants as a possibility.

    a. The household of Cornelius in Acts 10:1–2, and 48. "He and all his family were devout and God-fearing . . . so he ordered that they be baptized in the name of Jesus Christ." Notice they are called "devout and God-fearing." This would seem to exclude infants.

   b. The Philippian jailer's household in Acts 16:31–33. "They replied, 'Believe in the Lord Jesus and you will be saved—you and your household.' Then they spoke the word of the Lord to him and to all the others in his house... then immediately he and all his family were baptized." The instruction to "believe" would also seem to exclude infants.

   c. The household of Stephanas in 1 Corinthians 1:16. "Yes, I also baptized the household of Stephanas." It could be suggested from this verse that this house might possibly contain infants, but we have another reference to this household in 1 Corinthians 16:15. "You know that the household of Stephanas were the first converts in Achaia, and they have devoted themselves to the service of the saints." The phrase "devoted themselves" seems to limit this reference as well.

   d. The only other reference in Scripture is to the household of Lydia in Acts 16:14–15. It says that Lydia was "a worshiper of God" and "God opened her heart." No comment is made in this verse (one way or the other), about the age (whether there were infants) or a prerequisite response on the part of her family (did God also open their hearts?), only that they were baptized.

Finally, I believe (and everyone concurs), the overwhelming evidence of Scripture is to "believer's baptism."

   a. Matthew 28:19–20—we are to make disciples by baptizing and teaching.

   b. Mark 16:16—whoever believes and is baptized will be saved.

   c. Acts 2:38—repent and be baptized.

   d. Acts 8:34—baptism followed teaching.

   e. 1 Peter 3:21—baptism is the pledge of a clean conscience.

I hope this helps. Keep on asking questions. 1 Thessalonians 5:21 says, "Test everything. Hold on to what is good." That is certainly true of my teaching as well.

For further reading: *Baptism in the New Testament*, by G. R. Beasley-Murray.

EMAIL "Messages"

✉ INBOX [35/70]

To: Dr. Crane [eaglechristianchurch.com]
Subject: What Is the Proper Age for Baptism?

---Original Message---

When is the proper time for baptism for adults and children?

Reply:

I believe in believer's baptism. Simply said, baptism is for the believer who has repented of sin and confessed Christ and Lord and Savior.

Some churches practice infant baptism. The ceremony is intended to be a covenant between the parents and God on behalf of their child. The parents promise to raise their child in the faith until the child is old enough to make his own personal decision—at that time, the child is confirmed. This custom began several hundred years after the Bible was completed.

At the heart of the issue is the subject of sin. The doctrine of original sin as believed by the Catholic Church varies from most Protestant churches. We speak of reaching the "age of accountability" as being the determining factor. What do we mean by the "age of accountability"? It is the age when a child is able to consciously rebel against God. He recognizes what it is to be an enemy of God. That's when a person needs salvation and forgiveness. Baptism is for the believer who recognizes that he has offended God and wants to make peace through faith in Jesus Christ.

The baptism talked about in the New Testament was for those old enough to believe and repent of their sins. It was to be "the act of a good conscience toward God" (1 Peter 3:21). Usually a child understands the love of God (even the kind of intense love that would go to a cross) at an early age. What comes later, but is essential, is the understanding of sin as a personal offense to God. Sin is an abstract that is comprehended later than the understanding of love. Some churches have put the "age of accountability" at age eight. I have known some eight-year-olds who understood sufficiently; I have known others who did not. This important decision should not be rushed into or taken lightly. It should only be done for the right reasons and with the right motivation.

Many Christians come to our church from traditions involving infant baptism and subsequent confirmation. Their history does not include believers baptism. When someone from such a tradition comes to understand the command of Jesus in Matthew 28:19, we encourage them to be baptized in obedience to Jesus.

The New Testament pattern for new believers is that they are baptized immediately as they profess belief in Jesus as the Son of God and want to pledge their commitment to him as Lord and Savior.

EMAIL "Messages"

✉ INBOX [36/70]

To: Dr. Crane [eaglechristianchurch.com]
Subject: What Is the Proper Mode of Baptism?

---Original Message---

The faith tradition that I came from practiced baptism by sprinkling. I have noticed that your church (and others) perform baptisms much differently. Can you tell me what the proper mode of baptism is?

Reply:

The simplest answer to this question is found in the meaning of the word "baptize." Baptism comes from a Greek word which means to dip or to plunge (the word baptize is actually not a translation, but a transliteration). By definition, baptism is the act of immersion in water. Baptism by sprinkling (a practice that began hundreds of years after the establishment of the church) is self-contradictory—can you dip someone by sprinkling water on them?

At its very core, baptism depicts a believer's uniting with Christ's death, burial, and resurrection. Paul says, "Or don't you know that all of us who were baptized into Christ Jesus were baptized into his death? We were therefore buried with him through baptism into death in order that, just as Christ was raised from the dead through the glory of the Father, we too may live a new life" (Romans 6:3–4).

Being lowered into the water depicts dying to the old self and being buried with Christ. Coming out of the water illustrates Christ's resurrection and a believer's new life. Sprinkling (or pouring) fails to communicate these essential messages. Not only does baptism tell the story of what Christ has done for us, but it also illustrates our leaving our old life and becoming a new creation (2 Corinthians 5:17). It serves as our pledge of a clean conscience before God (1 Peter 3:21).

We encourage people to be immersed into Christ, even if they were baptized as an infant or sprinkled as an adult. Our hope is to faithfully follow Christ and his directives as closely as possible.

EMAIL "Messages"

✉ INBOX [37/70]

To: Dr. Crane [eaglechristianchurch.com]
Subject: What Is the Purpose of Mortal Life?

---Original Message---

As you know, I come from an LDS background where the purpose of life is couched in a very central notion of eternal progression. Mortal life is but a brief probationary state in the grand scheme of things on the way to godhood. Specifically, mortal life serves the following purpose: 1) to obtain a body; 2) to be tested, and 3) to receive all required priesthood ordinances (i.e., baptism, confirmation, temple washings/anointings, endowment, and sealings). Then, rather than being a "destination," the Celestial Kingdom is better described as a launching pad to eternity as a god. In an LDS framework, this puts moral life into a laser-like perspective as far as "purpose" goes. So what is the true purpose of mortal life?

Reply:

Thanks for the great question. You bring up many issues in this short paragraph, but let me tackle what I believe is your main question. I have tried to keep my answer brief—entire books have been written on "the meaning of life."

The Bible teaches that life begins at conception, and although man will exist eternally in the future (cf. heaven), we don't believe we have existed eternally in the past, but that God formed the soul of each man in the womb (Psalms 139:13; 31:15; Zechariah 12:1; etc). Man (Adam) was originally created for fellowship with God and placed in the garden (a taste of what heaven might be like) and knew only fellowship with God. But because of sin, that original fellowship with God was destroyed. God knew this would happen and in eternity past had already made provision for our salvation. God's plan for redemption included a type of relationship that could provide even deeper fellowship through his son, Jesus Christ. Those who accept Christ as their Savior can have fellowship with God as *their* choice, not simply because of a *de facto* relationship that existed with God in the beginning. Our purpose then, in this life, is to grow in our knowledge and love of Christ and to help other people do the same. While heaven is a gift from God that no one deserves or can earn; and while heaven will be given to all who accept Jesus as their Lord and Savior; we do believe that the Bible teaches rewards in heaven. These should not be confused with the "levels" of heaven that Mormonism teaches (this would require another conversation).

Allow me one "strange" analogy. I am not an avid golfer, but I play from time to time (I hack at the ball once or twice a year). But, if I got invited to go on an "all-expense-paid trip" to watch a Master's tournament, I would certainly enjoy watching these professional athletes compete. I would, however, probably not enjoy it as much as the person who spent their entire life studying and learning the intricacies of golf—who knew the golfers, the true difficulty of the course, and which holes favored each particular golfer. We (the novice and the expert) would both be enjoying the same tourney, but the other guy likely would appreciate it more. I believe the same thing is true of heaven. Heaven might very well be the same for everyone (you might not get a bigger condo than mine), but for those who have spent their entire life studying and serving God—they will be intricately more in tune with the enormity of God, the majesty of Jesus, and the beauty of heaven. The person who knows Christ intimately and has faithfully served him, will have a deeper appreciation (at least at the beginning of eternity in heaven) than the one who came to Christ at the eleventh hour (so to speak). That being said, there are tremendous advantages for those who serve diligently in this life. So our purpose here is to intimately know and serve God, and help others do the same, with the understanding that our eternal destinies are at stake.

For further reading on heaven: See *Surprised by Hope: Rethinking Heaven, the Resurrection and the Mission of the Church* by N.T. Wright. *Heaven* by Randy Alcorn. *The Purpose Driven Life* by Rick Warren has provided help for many Christians in their endeavor to find meaning and purpose in life.

Section Five

Bible Questions

EMAIL "Messages"

✉ INBOX [38/70]

To: Dr. Crane [eaglechristianchurch.com]
Subject: What about the Frequency of Communion?

---Original Message---

We have attended your services the last two weeks. We were pleasantly surprised when we came on what we thought was communion Sunday. We returned the next week and were curious when you served communion again. The tradition we were raised in only served communion once a quarter. Can we ask about the frequency in which you partake of the elements?

Reply:

It is great to have you worship with us! Please realize that the following discussion is not meant to be critical of others who may practice differently than we do. This simply serves as an explanation of "why" we do things the way we do.

As you have observed, we do practice communion every weekend! We believe that the Lord's Supper is an established practice initiated by Jesus to serve as a reminder of one's identification with Christ's death, burial, and his resurrection. We consider it a privilege and an expression of fellowship with the Lord and with one another.

Following the example of the believers in the book of Acts, we observe the Lord's Supper every Sunday. "On the first day of the week, we came together to break bread" (Acts 20:7). Acts 2:41–42 gives us this account: "Those who accepted his message were baptized . . . they devoted themselves to the apostles' teaching and to the fellowship, to the breaking of bread and to prayer."

But while we practice communion each Sunday, we do not limit it to Sunday worship. As we read through the New Testament, it appears that the earliest believers broke bread even more frequently (Acts 2:46)—always as a reminder of what Jesus had done for them. The elements themselves (bread and fruit of the vine) were common staples of the first century and thus served as daily pneumonic devices—constant reminders of Christ's sacrifice. Of course, we also remember that Jesus instituted the Lord's Supper on a Thursday night, before his arrest, crucifixion, and subsequent resurrection. Jesus' own words recorded for us in the New Testament simply say, "Whenever you eat this bread and drink this cup, you proclaim the Lord's death until he comes" (1 Corinthians 11:26).

Weekly communion (and even more frequent observance) certainly has the stamp of ancient practice, and we recommend it as a principle act of Christian worship. All ancient churches observe the Lord's Supper weekly—Catholic, Greek Orthodox, Coptic, Syrian Orthodox, etc. I can personally testify that after years of such practice, it has lost none of its meaning through frequent observance, but rather I long to have communion with my Lord and Savior as well as celebrate together with my brothers and sisters in Christ.

EMAIL "Messages"

✉ INBOX [39/70]

To: Dr. Crane [eaglechristianchurch.com]
Subject: What Is the Meaning of Communion?

---Original Message---

I heard you say during communion that it is not only a celebration of past events, but that it also has a present and future meaning. Can you please explain that to me?

Reply:

I do believe that communion touches the past, the present, and the future. Looking back, we are to remember Christ's atoning sacrifice on the cross. "The Lord Jesus, on the night he was betrayed, took bread, and when he had given thanks, he broke it and said, 'This is my body, which is for you; do this in remembrance of me.' In the same way, he took the cup, saying, 'This is the new covenant in my blood; do this, whenever you drink it, in remembrance of me'" (1 Corinthians 11:23–25).

In the present, we are to take spiritual inventory. In the Sermon on the Mount, Jesus taught that "if you are offering your gift at the altar and there remember that your brother has something against you, leave your gift there in front of the altar. First go and be reconciled to your brother; then come and offer your gift" (Matthew 5:23). In a similar vein, we are told that as we approach the Lord's Table, "A man ought to examine himself before he eats of the bread the drinks of the cup" (1 Corinthians 11:28). I like to pledge to God, "Lord, if there is anything that mars and scars the image of you in my life, make it known to me and help me rid myself of those things."

Communion also holds a future promise. "For whenever you eat this bread and drink this cup, you proclaim the Lord's death until he comes" (1 Corinthians 11:26). Did you notice the promise of Christ's future coming? The expression, "The Lord's Supper," brings to mind images of a great and glorious Messianic banquet to come. We can look forward with anticipation the day when Jesus comes again in power to receive his own people to himself, and where we will dine with Christ our King. Maranatha (Lord come quickly)!

EMAIL "Messages"

✉ INBOX [40/70]

To: Dr. Crane [eaglechristianchurch.com]
Subject: What about the Ten Commandments?

---Original Message---

If we are under the New Covenant and no longer under the Old Covenant, are the Ten Commandments still relevant or have they been replaced by something better?

Reply:

The answer to both of your questions is, "Yes." The Ten Commandments are still "relevant" to our world—extremely relevant. But the second part of your question is also true—the Ten Commandments have been replaced by something better.

At the heart of your question is the issue of salvation. Are we still under the Old Testament law (of which the Ten Commandments are a part)? The teaching of Scripture (including the teaching of the Old Testament itself, i.e. Jeremiah 31:31) is that the New Covenant fulfills the Old Covenant. Under the New Covenant, the emphasis is not on what we must do (law keeping), but on what Christ has done for us. The emphasis is not on the works we must perform, but on the righteousness Jesus is able to produce in us. By Jesus' perfect work on the cross, he has rescued and saved us from sin and his righteousness can be imputed to us. Salvation can only come one way: not through the law, but through the grace of Jesus Christ.

The Old Testament is still vitally important—we cannot understand the New Testament without the Old Testament. The concepts of sin, death, and sacrifice, as well as the understanding of Jesus

Christ as Messiah—all find their definition in the Old Testament. But while you cannot understand the New Testament without the Old Testament, it is also true that you cannot understand the Old Testament without the New Testament. The New Testament brings the fulfillment of the prophecies about Christ, the establishment of the church, and the promised way of salvation—not through works, but through the atoning sacrifice of Christ on the cross.

EMAIL "Messages"

✉ INBOX [41/70]

To: Dr. Crane [eaglechristianchurch.com]
Subject: What about Tithing?

---Original Message---

What does the Bible say about Christian tithing?

Reply:

Our relationship with God is meant to have a life-changing impact on every area of our life. This certainly includes our finances and possessions. That being said, it might surprise you to hear me say, "Tithing is an Old Testament concept." The tithe (meaning one-tenth) was a requirement of the law in which people were to give ten percent of everything they earned (Leviticus 27:30; Deuteronomy 14:24; 2 Chronicles 31:5). Actually, the Old Testament Law required multiple tithes, which would have pushed the total offering to be given under the Old Covenant beyond twenty percent.

Contrary to what some may teach, the New Testament nowhere commands (or even suggests) that Christians give a "tithe" out of obligation to a legalistic system. The Apostle Paul says, rather, that Christians should set aside a portion of their income (in keeping with their income) in order to support the church (1 Corinthians 16:1-2). The New Testament talks about the importance of giving, the benefits of giving, and about having right motives for our giving. The New Testament also gives example of people giving sacrificially, but is clear that the standard is, "Each man should give what he has decided in his heart to give, not reluctantly or under compulsion, for God loves a cheerful giver" (2 Corinthians 9:7).

While many have taken the ten-percent figure (tithe) and used it as a basis for a "recommended amount" for New Testament Christians—it should be viewed as a recommendation on their part. I would certainly suggest that you give and that you make it a practice to give generously and consistently. You should certainly heed the Bible's cautions against the love of money and practice the principles regarding its proper purpose and function. But most of all you should diligently pray and seek God's wisdom in the matter of how much you should give—it may be ten percent, it may be more, it may be that you start small and build up as God leads you forward.

Jesus said, "Do not store up for yourselves treasures on earth, where moth and rust destroy, and where thieves break in and steal. But store up for yourselves treasures in heaven, where moth and rust do not destroy, and where thieves do not break in and steal. For where your treasure is, there your heart will be also" (Matthew 6:19–21).

EMAIL "Messages"

✉ INBOX [42/70]

To: Dr. Crane [eaglechristianchurch.com]
Subject: What Is Expository Preaching?

---Original Message---

I keep hearing that Eagle Christian Church practices expository preaching. Can you please explain to me what this means?

Reply:

"Exposition" is related to the word "expose." The expository preacher's goal is simply to expose the meaning of the Bible, verse by verse, usually making his way through a Bible book or a biblical passage. His goal is to communicate the intended meaning of the passage to a modern audience. Our normal habits include preaching through an entire book of the Bible, verse by verse and chapter by chapter.

To prepare an expository sermon, the preacher starts with a passage of Scripture and then studies the grammar, the context, and the historical setting of the passage to better understand the author's original intent. In other words, the expositor is trying to find the intended meaning to the intended audience. Only after he understands the meaning of a particular passage can he craft a sermon to explain and apply it.

Expository preaching differs from a topical sermon where the preacher starts with a topic of his own choosing and then may (or may not) find Bible verses that speak to this topic. It also differs from a textual sermon where a preacher uses a particular text to make a point without examining the original intent of the text.

While expository preaching is not the only valid way to preach, it is by far the best for teaching the plain sense of the Bible and should be the mainstay of a churches' preaching. Expository preaching carries with it the safeguards of preaching the Bible faithfully and consistently—a safeguard other methods might fail to employ. The goal of expository preaching is for everyone involved to understand what Bible passages mean and therefore understand what God requires of them.

For further information: *Biblical Preaching* by Haddon Robinson.

EMAIL "Messages"

✉ INBOX [43/70]

To: Dr. Crane [eaglechristianchurch.com]
Subject: What about Cremation?

---Original Message---

During a recent funeral of a friend, an urn was set where we expected the casket. Afterwards, my mother seemed to be upset that this Christian man had been cremated. This brought about a heated discussion at our house. Can I ask you, "Is it okay for a Christian to be cremated?"

Reply:

Throughout recorded history, people have generally disposed of the physical remains of their dead by either burying them or burning them. If cremated—fire turns the body to ashes. If decomposed in the ground—time turns the body into the dust of the earth. It seems that cremation simply speeds up the process. Abraham acknowledged the ultimate demise of the body thousands of years ago when he said, "I am nothing but dust and ashes" (Genesis 18:27).

There are some Christians who oppose cremation because they consider it an impediment to resurrection. But God, who created all things to begin with, can easily raise the dead no matter how they died and no matter how their bodies were disposed of. It seems to me that if God can deliver people from fire while they are alive (Daniel 3), he can do the same after they have died. We do know that both Saul and Jonathan were cremated (1 Samuel 13:31).

I am confident that those whose bodies were lost at sea, those whose bodies were destroyed in automobile accidents, and the bodies of 3,000 who died in the Twin Towers on 9/11 will pose no problem for our Creator God who made us out of dust to begin with (Genesis 2:7). The Christian martyrs who died by being burnt at the stake, those who were dipped in tar and used to light the Roman Coliseum, and even those who were eaten by lions are also safe in God's keeping.

Scripture leaves some mystery regarding the resurrection, but although our new bodies will be seemingly recognizable, the body that will be raised will be qualitatively different from the body we had on earth (1 Corinthians 15:41–54).

One last thing: as Christians we should ultimately remember that our physical bodies are not the real "us." Our bodies are merely earthly tents for our dwelling here; our ultimate home is with God. On the day of my demise, do not mourn, I will have gone to a better place. A cardboard box or a hot furnace will not change that reality.

EMAIL "Messages"

✉ INBOX [44/70]

To: Dr. Crane [eaglechristianchurch.com]
Subject: Is Suicide Unforgivable?

---Original Message---

I have heard it said that a true Christian would never commit suicide and that it is a sin which God does not forgive. Is this true?

Reply:

This is an issue that has directly affected me and my family. I, too, have had "Christian" people make similar comments regarding the nature of suicide. I must say their remarks seemed ungracious, uncalled for, and unsympathetic.

While Scripture tells us that God is the author of life and that each human life is precious—I know of no passage in the Bible which says directly or indirectly that suicide is a sin. I know of Biblical passages that tell us not to murder. I know of Biblical passages which record the stories of those who have committed suicide. But I am unfamiliar with any passage that does more than simply state the historical facts surrounding the deaths of those involved, or relate to us that the body is to be used to honor God (1 Corinthians 6:19–20).

Let me acknowledge that suicide is without a doubt a horrible tragedy and the source of untold grief (both to God and man). Suicide is the cause of a multitude of problems and has long-term, lasting consequences on the lives of family and friends. Suicide should likely even make our lists of "sins"—but still I cannot (and will not) say that suicide places a person outside the grace of God.

Scripturally, the only "unforgivable sin" is the consistent, intentional, and ongoing rejection of God's grace.

It might help to mention the source of this unfortunate doctrine of suicide as "the unforgivable sin." Roman Catholicism limits divine grace to the "sacraments," and based on this (not Scripture), they have concluded that a suicide victim (who cannot gain penance from a priest) is beyond God's help and reach.

Personally, I have known committed Christians who have taken their own lives in a moment of unclear thinking and desperation. In some instances, these people truly believed they were doing their family, friends, and even church a favor. While suicide is obviously wrong, I cannot with good conscience say that those who have taken their own lives in a moment of darkness and desperation, have somehow severed themselves from the abundant grace of our Lord and Savior, Jesus Christ.

EMAIL "Messages"

✉ INBOX [45/70]

To: Dr. Crane [eaglechristianchurch.com]
Subject: What about Guardian Angels?

---Original Message---

Do Christians (people) have guardian angels?

Reply:

There is certainly a great deal of interest in angels these days, but most of what we hear is disconnected from biblical material. The pictures we see of angels on clouds with harps, halos, wings, and Cupid's arrows are mostly glorified imagination. But your question has merit. The notion that people have guardian angels is loosely based on Scripture and comes primarily from Matthew 18:10, which reads: "See that you do not look down on one of these little ones. For I tell you that their angels in heaven always see the face of my Father in heaven."

Once generally confined to angels watching over children, the belief in "guardian angels" has taken on a life of its own. It is now prevalent to find the belief that everyone (man, woman, and child) has a "protecting angel" guarding them. Stories of angels assisting people are the basis, not only of humorous TV commercials, but popular network dramas. One Christian artist, Amy Grant, sang the hit song, *Angels Watching Over Me*.

Let me start by saying, it is certainly true that God has used angels to intervene on behalf of people throughout history. Daniel and his friends, Shadrach, Meshach, and Abednego, were all rescued by an angel from the fiery furnace (Daniel 3:28). An angel shut the mouths of Daniel's lions (Daniel 6:22). Peter was released from prison by an angel (Acts 12:7-10). The Bible also says that angels provide protection for humans on occasion (Psalms 34:7; 2 Kings 6:8-23). Somehow, and in some way, angels give assistance to Christian people. The writer of Hebrews says: "Are not all angels ministering spirits sent to serve those who will inherit salvation?" (Hebrews 1:14).

Certainly, it is biblical for us to believe that angels can and have provided protection for people on occasion. But should this be our expectation? Are we each promised a protecting angel? If the popular view of "guardian angels" is correct, we must ask why angels don't intervene more often—especially when we consider the unspeakable crimes and abuses that are perpetrated against children. Has Jesus' promised protection for children (Matthew 18:10) fallen short? Or is something else in play? I would submit that Jesus doesn't promise intervention or protection, but that the angels in heaven take note of all crimes and abuses against "the little ones" and those abuses are ever before "the face of my Father in heaven." God's knowledge of abuse will be used by him in future judgment. This seems to better reflect what the passage actually says and also allows for the reality that abuses often occur.

While it is proper for us to recognize the existence and ministry of angels, we must be careful not to "glorify" angels or assign to them responsibilities which are unwarranted by Scripture. Paul warned that "worshiping angels" and focusing too much on them is one way to get off-track (Colossians 2:18-19). The Apostle John was repeatedly reminded that he was not to focus his devotion on the angel assisting him (Revelation 1:1; 19:10; 22:8-9). We should acknowledge the existence of angels, but worship Christ.

EMAIL "Messages"

✉ INBOX [46/70]

To: Dr. Crane [eaglechristianchurch.com]
Subject: What about Other Inhabited Worlds?

---Original Message---

Do you believe that it is possible that God may have created other worlds in addition to Earth, or do you believe Earth is the only planet inhabited by God's creations?

Reply:

My honest answer is, "I dunno!" The Bible makes no claim one way or the other. To give a definitive answer is to speak where the Bible doesn't speak. I would answer that it is certainly possible that God could create another universe with an inhabitable planet, but we get no clear indication of this anywhere in Scripture. This is not to say that some might find obscure passages that they use to posit the possibility (cf. Genesis 6:1–4). Mormonism would certainly make the claim that there are other worlds along with other gods whose job is to populate those planets. This belief, however, does not find its source in the Bible.

My own personal opinion: I have met a few people I thought were from different planets!

Section Six

Bible Difficulties

EMAIL "Messages"

✉ INBOX [47/70]

To: Dr. Crane [eaglechristianchurch.com]
Subject: Where Did Cain Get His Wife?

---Original Message---

Where did Cain get his wife?

Reply:

This specific question, along with a second, "Did Adam have a belly button?" are among the most frequently asked questions from Genesis. This first question actually involves a much larger question: what other people existed besides Adam and Eve?

According to Genesis, at some point in his life, Cain murdered his younger brother Abel (4:8). His punishment resulted in banishment from the land (4:14). Three verses later, however, we see Cain, not only married and expecting a child, but building a city (4:17). How does one account for this?

Some suggest that God created another race and placed them on earth, but this is not a tenable solution. The Bible clearly teaches us that Adam was the first man (1 Corinthians 15:45) and that his wife, Eve, was "the mother of all living" (Genesis 3:20).

The key to answering this question is the fact that Genesis nowhere indicates at what point in the life of Cain he murdered his brother, married a wife, or built his city. Even a few hundred years might have passed before all the events recorded in this chapter took place.

Genesis 5:4 does tell us that Adam had other sons and daughters. Cain must have married a sister or a niece or even grand niece.

If you consider the length of life recorded for us in the book of Genesis (around 900 years on average, Adam lived 930), a very sizeable population could have developed very rapidly. Using a conservative approximation, scholars suggest that there could have been more than one million people living by the death of Cain.

Some might balk at this answer, suggesting that if this is the case, Cain must have committed incest which the Bible condemns (Leviticus 18:6) and this practice often produces genetic defects in children. But there were no genetic imperfections at the beginning. Genetic defects resulted from the Fall and only occurred gradually over time. Further, the command to not marry within family lines does not come until the time of Moses which is thousands of years later.

As for whether or not Adam had a belly button, I speculate that he must have—when God pulled him out of the oven, he poked him and said, "Yep, he's done!"

EMAIL "Messages"

✉ INBOX [48/70]

To: Dr. Crane [eaglechristianchurch.com]
Subject: What Is the Mark of Cain?

---Original Message---

In the church I used to attend, I was taught that the "Mark of Cain" was a reference to the color of skin that was given to him due to his disobedience. Is that true?

Reply:

Having grown up in Salt Lake City, I am aware of this type of teaching. I remember hearing one radio talk show host who was promoting this very issue when a lady called in who was obviously from the deep South. Her response was rather humorous. She said something to the effect of, "We believe God turned Cain white!"

When Paul, in the book of Acts, was having a lively discussion with a group of Stoic philosophers around the Areopagus in Athens, he spoke of the one true God who made *all the nations* from one common ancestor. "From one man he made every nation of men" (Acts 17:26).

The book of Genesis gives us a much more detailed account. From Adam and Eve came every human being. There are not many races, there is only one race—the human race. Over the years, because of climate, food, and genetics, we have developed physical distinctions. The color of our skin was not a mark placed on anyone by God.

Cain, after he murdered his brother, was banished by God and given a "mark" to prevent anyone from killing him to avenge Abel's death (Genesis 4:13–15). This mark was unique to him. Nothing is said about it being hereditary! Furthermore, whatever mark Cain was given was actually a mark of divine protection and not one of divine punishment. Some (can I say ignorant?) people have attempted to justify racial discrimination (even in religious circles) by claiming that the mark of Cain was the color of his skin.

We should also remember, years after Cain and Abel, God destroyed the world by a flood. After the flood, the human race descended (not from Cain or Abel) but from Noah's three sons (Ham, Shem, and Japheth) and their wives (Genesis 7). Biblical genealogies show that Ham's descendants moved to the regions of North Africa (Egypt) and Mesopotamia (Genesis 9:18). Descendants of Shem became the Israelites and the Semitic people. It is thought that Japheth became the father of the European nations.

It is also interesting that the "oldest ancestor of China" is one they refer to as "Oah of the great flood." The oldest Chinese dynasty dates to a period just after the biblical time of the flood (do I need to remind you that Noah lived more than 100 years beyond the time of the flood?).

You see, there are not many races, there is just one race—the human race!

EMAIL "Messages"

✉ INBOX [49/70]

To: Dr. Crane [eaglechristianchurch.com]
Subject: Why Aren't Dinosaurs Mentioned in the Bible?

---Original Message---

Why aren't dinosaurs mentioned in the Bible?

Reply:

The term "dinosaur" was actually coined by a famous paleontologist named Richard Owen in 1841. This was nearly eighteen centuries after the New Testament was finished and two centuries after the King James Bible was translated in 1611.

Actually, the Bible does mention creatures that many believe to be dinosaurs. Let me give you two from what may be the oldest book in the Bible. Job mentions the Behemoth and Leviathan. Behemoth is described as having a tail like a cedar tree. "Look at the behemoth, which I made along with you and feeds on grass like an ox. What strength he has . . . what power . . . His tail sways like a cedar . . . His bones are tubes of bronze, his limbs like rods of iron. He ranks first among the works of God" (Job 40:15–19).

Leviathan is pictured with scales, terrible teeth, and is so fierce that no one dare wake him up. (Job 41:9–10, 13–15). Some older versions of the Bible call them "dragons." It is easy to see why many Bible scholars have concluded that Leviathan and Behemoth may have been dinosaurs.

This often leads to a second commonly asked question about dinosaurs. How did the dinosaurs become extinct? The short answer is—the same way we account for the other tens to hundreds of thousands (some would say one million) of other species over the centuries that have gone extinct due to a combination of changing ecosystems (including the flood) and the domination of predators (including man).

EMAIL "Messages"

✉ INBOX [50/70]

To: Dr. Crane [eaglechristianchurch.com]
Subject: If God Hardened Pharaoh's Heart, Did He Have Free Will?

---Original Message---

I read in Exodus chapter four that God hardened Pharaoh's heart. If God hardened Pharaoh's heart, didn't God override Pharaoh's free will? I guess what I am asking is, if God hardened Pharaoh's heart, how can Pharaoh be held accountable?

Reply:

A close look at Exodus chapters seven through nine is revealing. The Bible makes it very clear that Pharaoh was responsible for the hardening of his own heart. Seven times we read that he "hardened his own heart" or that his heart "grew hard" (7:13, 22; 8:15, 19, 32; 9:7, 35).

God did not harden Pharaoh's heart contrary to Pharaoh's own free choice. It is true that God made a prediction that this would happen (4:21), but Pharaoh hardened his own heart before God hardened it later (9:12; 10:1, 20, 27).

We should remember in our own lives, that if we harden our heart repeatedly against God, there is a point at which God will give up on us.

This same issue comes up again in Romans 9:17.

EMAIL "Messages"

✉ INBOX [51/70]

To: Dr. Crane [eaglechristianchurch.com]
Subject: What Are the Nephilim?

---Original Message---

I read in Genesis 6:1–2 about the sons of God marrying the daughters of men. The Bible says that their offspring were Nephilim. Can you help me out here?

Reply:

The opening verses of Genesis 6 are obviously difficult. As you have pointed out, two phrases, "sons of God" and "Nephilim," are at the center of the issue. There are several different views regarding this issue. Let me explain briefly.

Sons of God
1. The phrase "sons of God" is often used to refer to angels (Job 1:6; 2:1; 38:7) causing some to think that angels married humans and their offspring were giants (Nephilim). However, Matthew 22:30 (cf. Mark 12:25) tells us that angels "neither marry nor are given in marriage." Thus, our passage here cannot refer to angels. One should also pay attention to the punishment God doles out: "I will wipe mankind, whom I have created, from the face of the earth—men and animals, and creatures that move along the ground, and birds of the air—for I am grieved that I have made them." One would expect that if the angels had participated in this event, they along with mankind, would have received punishment. The fact that the angels are not subject to punishment gives even

further weight to the conclusion that they are not the "sons of God" mentioned in 6:1.

2. Some believe that phrase "sons of God" refers to great men of old (men of renown) or kings. Some (not all) holding this view believe that the ten men mentioned in chapter 5 are given long life as a gift of God and for this reason are called the sons of God. While these views are possible from verse 4, they are probably not the best choice.

3. I believe that the best explanation is that the "sons of God" are those men who had previously remained faithful to God, but began to intermarry with those who had not. (The fact that marriage began to erode is clearly the point of this passage.) These "sons of God" may have been descendants of Seth who indiscriminately married women (possibly from the lineage of Cain) who did not share the values God required of his people. There is no doubt that godly people are often called "sons of God" (and daughters of God) in Scripture. Here, the sons of God married superficially because of the physical attraction to these women rather than giving consideration to their godliness: "They married any of them they chose" (v. 2). God's wrath was poured out on them for their unfaithfulness to his principles (see verses 3, 5). This is no different than being "unequally yoked" in the New Testament (2 Corinthians 6:14).

Those of righteous background married those of unrighteous background. In a different culture, it could have as easily been stated the daughters of God (righteous) married the sons of man (the unrighteous).

Most of the confusion over "Sons of God" actually stems, not from this phrase itself, but the next phrase, "*Nephilim*." If this was not in the text, our reading would only be natural.

Nephilim

Many refer to the *Nephilim* as "giants." The NIV footnote in the Life Application Bible says, "*Nephilim* refers to a powerful race of giants . . . probably nine or ten feet tall." They come to this conclusion because the same word *"Nephilim"* is used in Numbers 13:33 of people who made the Israelites look like grasshoppers in their own eyes. Also, we find Goliath in 1 Samuel 17, who was over 9 feet tall. Combining these three verses, some conclude that since Goliath was 9 feet tall, and since the *Nephilim* in the book of Numbers were tall, the *Nephilim* in Genesis were also 9 feet tall (along with the assumption that they were offspring of angels).

While the *Nephilim* in the book of Numbers were tall (we don't know how tall), the *Nephilim* in the book of Numbers are not and cannot be descendants of those mentioned in Genesis (remember the flood?). Also, the Genesis account cannot be twisted to suggest that the *Nephilim* were the product of angels (see above) nor does the text say that the *Nehphilim* were even the children of the sons of God and daughters of men. It only tells us that they were around during and after that period of time (v. 4). The text is not clear if the *Nephilim* were the product of the marriages just mentioned; contemporary with the marriages just mentioned (but separate from), or if they were considered "the mighty men of old" who were at one time, "men of renown" but who had turned corrupt. While the *Nephilim* in the book of Numbers were obviously tall, the word *Nephilim* does not so much mean "giant" (KJV) as "tyrant." The word comes from the Hebrew root meaning "to fall upon." (It is also significant to note that the *Nephilim* could also be called "the fallen ones.") What did the *"Nephilim"* in Genesis (however tall they were), their counterparts in the book of Numbers (we know they were tall), and the 9-foot Goliath have in common? They were all bullies, or at least powerful men gone bad. *Nephilim* are simply bullies who "fell upon" others to force their will upon them. Their violence is emphasized in verse 11—"The earth was corrupt in God's sight and full of violence."

God did not regret creating humanity. He was expressing sorrow for what the people had done—like a parent might express sorrow over a rebellious child. God was sorry that people chose sin rather than a relationship with him.

EMAIL "Messages"

✉ INBOX [52/70]

To: Dr. Crane [eaglechristianchurch.com]
Subject: Is Sunday the Sabbath?

---Original Message---

Why do we observe the Sabbath on Sunday while the Jews observe the Sabbath on Saturday?

Reply:

The Sabbath has always been Saturday. God commanded Israel at Mount Sinai (Exodus 20:8–11; Deuteronomy 5:12–15) to observe the Sabbath as a day of rest for several reasons. It was not only to commemorate God's own seventh-day rest during Creation (Genesis 2:2), but also a day to remember their liberation from slavery (Deuteronomy 5:15). Contrary to popular opinion, the Jewish Sabbath was a day of rest—not a day of public worship. When first-century Jews accepted Jesus as Messiah, they continued to observe the Sabbath day as they had always done.

It is worth mentioning that the Sabbath was never given to non-Jews, and the New Testament does not designate any particular day as holy day for followers of Christ. Some Christians through the centuries have mistakenly called Sunday "the Christian Sabbath," but the Bible never uses that kind of language.

The reason Christians often worship on Sunday is because they are celebrating the resurrection of Jesus Christ which happened on the first day of the week. Most Christians generally accept Sunday to be the Lord's Day mentioned in Revelation 1:10. We see in Scripture that God's people often met together on the first day of the week (though not exclusively) for communion (Acts 20:7), to set aside special offerings (1 Corinthians 16:1ff), and for corporate worship. Although Christian believers have regularly met on Sundays for 2,000 years, the Bible tells us that the particular day on which one honors God is not of primary importance (Romans 14:5ff; Colossians 2:16). We should rejoice in God's presence seven days a week, and we may worship him at any time we feel called to do so.

As Christians, we are not bound by the Sabbath, but there is nothing wrong with enjoying a day of rest when an open Saturday (or another day) rolls around.

EMAIL "Messages"

✉ INBOX [53/70]

To: Dr. Crane [eaglechristianchurch.com]
Subject: What about Modern-day Apostles?

---Original Message---

The church from which I came claims to have apostles. Are there still apostles today?

Reply:

The word "apostle" (*apostolos*) literally means "delegate" or "one sent out." In a generic way, it could be argued that this word could be applied to anyone sent out from the church. But in the Bible, its use is much more limited.

In its highest use, the word is used of Jesus as the supreme apostle. The writer of Hebrews says, "Fix your thoughts on Jesus, the apostle and high priest" (Hebrews 3:1). Of course we know that God sent Jesus into the world with authority to make atonement for sin and offer eternal life (John 17:1-3).

Normally, in Scripture, when the word "apostle" is used it refers to the Twelve Apostles. They were men who were appointed by Jesus (with Matthias replacing Judas after his death) and who possessed a special and unique role in the Church. They were all men who had been with Jesus, beginning with John's baptism, and remained with him throughout his death, burial, and resurrection (Acts 1:21-22). The Twelve Apostles performed feats that verified who they were: "the things that mark an apostle—signs, wonders and miracles—were done among you with great perseverance" (2 Corinthians 12:12).

Paul also was an apostle in the same sense as the Twelve—though he calls himself an apostle "abnormally born" (1 Corinthians 15:8). Throughout Scripture, he frequently defends his apostleship and insists that his standing is in no way inferior (1 Corinthians 9:1; 1 Timothy 2:7) having also been commissioned by Jesus (Romans 1:1; Galatians 1:1; Ephesians 1:1; Colossians 1:1). Paul served as "the apostle to the Gentiles" (Romans 11:13).

Although the Bible's normal use of the word "apostle" refers to the Twelve and Paul, the New Testament does recognize (on rare occasion) some other individuals. Andronicus and Junias are said to be "outstanding among the apostles" (Romans 16:7), and Paul seems to include Barnabas as an apostle when he says "Don't we have the right to food and drink . . . as do the other apostles . . . or is it only I and Barnabas who must work for a living (1 Corinthians 9:1–6). To my knowledge, the use of "apostle" stops here.

I have no doubt that God still commissions people for his service. We are all aware of people who are "apostolic" in the missionary sense of being "sent out" by the church (like Barnabas, Andronicus, and Junias). I would be careful, however, of anyone who considered themselves an "apostle" in more than this generic sense. I would certainly squirm if someone claimed to be an apostle like a Peter, James, or John!

To this point, twice in Scripture, the New Testament writers warn against false apostles and people who claim to have spiritual authority equal to the Twelve: "For such men are false apostles, deceitful workmen, masquerading as apostles of Christ" (2 Corinthians 11:13); and, "I know that you cannot tolerate wicked men, that you have tested those who claim to be apostles but are not, and have found them false" (Revelation 2:2).

I would reject any false claim of authority, whether such apostleship was said to have been transmitted by a special chain of succession, or if the claim were that "apostleship" was re-manifested on earth after centuries of absence, in order to restore the one true church.

EMAIL "Messages"

✉ INBOX [54/70]

To: Dr. Crane [eaglechristianchurch.com]
Subject: What about Spiritual Gifts?

---Original Message---

What do you believe about Spiritual Gifts?

Reply:

No other theology within the church has caused more division than the subject of spiritual gifts. Anything that causes division is sin. Some believe ALL of the spiritual gifts spoken of in 1 Corinthians 12–14 are for today. Many believe SOME of the gifts are for today, some believe NONE of the gifts are for today. You can see the potential for problems. I do not believe that this subject constitutes a salvation issue and should not split the church—we can have a difference of opinion about this and both be Christians.

That being said, here is where I stand, specifically on the issue of speaking in tongues (which seems to be the most outward and debatable of the issues). First, I believe the Spirit of God does not work contrary to the Word of God (see 1 John 4:1–6). Second, I do not personally practice speaking in tongues. I believe this was one of the gifts given for the immediate confirmation and proclamation of the gospel of Jesus Christ (Acts 2) and not a gift given to all believers. Third, I take seriously the specific rules for the use of this gift that must be followed if a person (or church) claims to have this gift. I believe these were put in place because the church in Corinth was experiencing problems over this very issue and tongue speaking was dividing the church. Here are the God-given biblical mandates:

1. If someone speaks in a tongue it will be one at a time (1 Corinthians 14:27).
2. There must be an interpreter (1 Corinthians 14:28).
3. There must be one who discerns whether it comes from God (1 John 4:1).
4. It will not be done in a public assembly (1 Corinthians 14:23).
5. If it is a prayer language, there is a place to pray (Matthew 6:6).
6. The gifts must be used to edify the church, not the individual (1 Corinthians 14:4).
7. No one has all the gifts, but the church is to be a body (1 Corinthians 12:27–30).

I know of few churches who are practicing "tongues" and accurately following these biblical guidelines.

EMAIL "Messages"

✉ INBOX [55/70]

To: Dr. Crane [eaglechristianchurch.com]
Subject: What about Homosexuality?

---Original Message---

What does the Bible say about the practice of homosexuality? It seems some Christians accept it; others excuse it as an illness; still others openly preach against it. One church in town has a minister who openly practices this lifestyle.

Reply:

As Christians, there are two principles we always need to remember. The first principle is that love is at the very core of Christianity. We are to love all people regardless of their race, gender, background, lifestyle, or whether they agree with us or not. Jesus said, "Love one another. As I have loved you, so you must love one another. By this all men will know that you are my disciples, if you love one another" (John 13:34–35). We are commanded to love. Lack of love is a violation of the very essence of who we are to be as Christians. It is a sad fact that many reflect great animosity towards their fellow man/woman.

Our second reminder is that each one of us finds himself in the same predicament—we are all sinners in need of grace. As Christians, there is no room for any hint of self-righteousness or a "holier-than-thou" attitude. "All have sinned and fall short of the glory of God" (Romans 3:23). All of us stand unworthy and undeserving before a holy God. Thank God for his mercy, forgiveness, and acceptance of us as sinners.

Having said that, the Bible is clear about the practice of homosexuality (1 Corinthians 6:9; Romans 1:26-27). It is a sin—just like other sins—no more, no less. Some (even Christians) try wrongly to justify it. Others (even preachers) try to excuse it. Some even claim that a person's sexual preference is innate and therefore given, approved, and blessed by God. But all who call for cultural acceptance do so at the expense of clear Biblical teaching.

Let me switch gears for just a moment. I am told that some people are so predisposed toward alcohol that they can become an alcoholic from the very first drink. Would anyone suggest that because a person has alcoholic tendencies we should tolerate (even for a moment) their drunkenness? I know some people are more predisposed towards anger—does this tendency towards violence justify child or spousal abuse? I would daresay that every one of us, in some way, is hard-wired with a specific craving or passion that if followed would lead us into sin. Does that craving justify our sinfulness?

While certain people might have homosexual tendencies, this does not justify homosexual behavior. You will not find any New Testament imperative that normalizes or even tolerates this lifestyle. There is no way to honestly contort or compromise Biblical teaching in a manner that rightly justifies homosexual behavior. None. That being said, the Bible does not condemn the practice of homosexuality as the worst of all sins. It is a sin—no more, no less. The Bible also thankfully teaches that every sinner: the sexually immoral, the idolater, the adulterer, the prostitute, the homosexual, the thief, the greedy, the drunkard, the slanderer, the swindler—all can be saved through Jesus Christ. "[For] that is what some of you were. But you were washed, you were sanctified, you were justified in the name of the Lord Jesus Christ and by the Spirit of our God" (1 Corinthians 6:11).

Section Seven

Questions about Eschatology (The End Times)

EMAIL "Messages"

✉ INBOX [56/70]

To: Dr. Crane [eaglechristianchurch.com]
Subject: What about the Battle of Armageddon?

---Original Message---

I have been reading various books which all say something different about the Battle of Armageddon. Can you explain to me what is going on?

Reply:

The topic of Armageddon has been at the heart of countless sermons, lectures, and books for the last 50 years. In order to understand this battle, we need to review the Old Testament where the story is rooted.

We find the key to this imagery in Judges chapters 4 and 5. Israel is in misery again. This particular time, King Jabin (a Canaanite) is the one oppressing Israel. His people have been plundering the fields and crops of Israel. His men are so violent that the Israelites are afraid to even be out in the open. The Israelites are out-manned and out-armed by the Canaanites. General Sisera has nine hundred iron chariots (4:12), while Israel has barely a spear among them.

But along comes Deborah. She tells Barak the Judge (despite appearances to the contrary) that God is on Israel's side. "Go! This day the Lord has given Sisera into your hands. Has not the Lord gone ahead of you?" (4:14). Israel (with the help of Jael, Heber's wife—who drives a tent peg through Sisera's head) handily defeats the Canaanites (4:21).

This battle at Armageddon (a very small battlefield near the city of Megiddo—southeast of Haifa in Northern Israel) becomes a symbol of every battle in which, when the need is the greatest and believers are oppressed, the Lord reveals his power and defeats the enemy. Many battles throughout Scripture replay this scenario—God rescuing his people when the situation seems bleakest.

Before the final "Armageddon," it may appear that Satan and his forces will be victorious, but when the need is the greatest, and when God's children are oppressed on every side; Christ will appear suddenly to deliver his people. It is for this reason that the imagery of the battle of Armageddon is the sixth bowl in Revelation 16:16. The seventh bowl is judgment day.

Like other Old Testament illustrations before it, Armageddon pictures many events throughout history, but reaches its final and most complete realization just before, and in connection with the last day.

EMAIL "Messages"

✉ INBOX [57/70]

To: Dr. Crane [eaglechristianchurch.com]
Subject: What about the Antichrist?

---Original Message---

Hi Steve. My wife and I are new to the church the past couple of months. We have joined a small group and it has been nothing but a positive experience for my family. I had a quick question to bounce off of you: How aware are you of Javier Solana? From what I understand, he is part of the European Recommendation and currently sits in the seat number marked 666. There are speculations about him being the Antichrist. I think he has been a part of the European Recommendation for a long time, and is supposedly one of the most powerful people in the world. If this is true, it would seem that people would be aware of a person of such great political power. The gradual popularity seems to mirror where the Antichrist is said to come from. Also, I think his lineage is from the Roman Catholic Church and I think that also mirrors prophecy of the Antichrist. I am in no way claiming to know anything about Javier besides from the different articles I've read. I am sure there is a lot more information that I don't know about. I just wanted to get your take on the whole subject. Shouldn't people know about him? Thank you for your time and God bless.

Reply:
It's great to have you as part of our family. I am glad to hear that you have plugged into a small group. There is always much speculation about the number "666" and "the Antichrist." I have heard speculations pointing to everyone from Hitler, Mussolini, Gorbachev,

Kissinger, Reagan, Khadafi, Saddat, Bush, Bin Laden, Kim Jong-il, Castro, and now Obama. While Revelation talks about the number of the beast (666, Revelation 13:18), it is interesting that the word "antichrist" is not used in the book of Revelation. In fact, antichrist is only found four times in all of Scripture. I would challenge you to look up three verses where all four uses of antichrist are found and ask two questions: "Who is the antichrist?" and "How many are there?" Here are the uses of antichrist: 1 John 2:18 (2x); 1 John 2:22; 1 John 4:2–3; 2 John 7.

God bless you, Steve.

EMAIL "Messages"

✉ INBOX [58/70]

To: Dr. Crane [eaglechristianchurch.com]
Subject: When Are the Last Days?

---Original Message---

Do you believe that we are living in the last days?

Reply:

Yes! And we have been for some time! The last days are not just in the distant future, but were actually inaugurated at Pentecost (cf. Acts 2:17; 1 Corinthians 10:11). The phrase "last days" (plural) in the New Testament always refers to the time between Christ's first and second coming (Acts 2:17; 2 Timothy 3:1; Hebrews 1:2; James 5:3; 2 Peter 3:3). The term "last day" (singular) refers to a day of judgment at the end of the last days (John 6:39, 40, 44, 45; 11:24; 12:48).

Let me quote two of these passages for you with a little background. The first comes from the Book of Acts regarding an event called Pentecost. This was the day that the church was started. The Holy Spirit had just descended upon the Apostles with what appeared to be tongues of fire and they were able to speak with every person present understanding in their own native language (dialect). Peter then stood up and explained that the events they were all witnessing were actually a fulfillment of what was spoken by the prophet Joel: "In the last days, God says, I will pour out my Spirit" (Acts 2:17). He explained to them that what had long been predicted in the Old Testament had now occurred in their presence and that they were living in the last days—the time of the Messiah.

A second passage reinforces this point. The writer of Hebrews says, "In the past God spoke to our forefathers through the prophets at many times and in various ways, but in these last days he has spoken to us by his Son" (Hebrews 1:1–2). God revealed himself through the prophets in the past, but now he not only has spoken through his Son, but his final way of dealing with mankind is through Jesus Christ.

We are all living in the last days (plural) which will lead up to the last day (singular). These are the last days of salvation (2 Corinthians 6:2) which will lead up to the day of salvation and wrath (1 Thessalonians 5:1–11).

To bring this point home, the following expressions in Scripture are all equivalent for the "last days" (the period of time between Jesus' death and resurrection and the final judgment):

"The last days" (Acts 2:17; 2 Timothy 3:1; Hebrews 1:2; James 5:3; 2 Peter 3:3)

"The last hour" (1 John 2:18)

"The last time" (Jude 18)

"The last times" (1 Peter 1:20)

EMAIL "Messages"

✉ INBOX [59/70]

To: Dr. Crane [eaglechristianchurch.com]
Subject: What Is the Tribulation?

---Original Message---

I hear some Christians talk about the tribulation. What are they talking about?

Reply:

Many Christians have fretted about a period of tribulation that they believe comes at the end of the age. This particular belief is propagated by those who teach what is called "premillenialism" (a belief that Christ's return is preceded by a seven-year period of tribulation followed by a thousand year millennium). It should be pointed out that this teaching has only been around for the last 150 years and only gained popularity in the last fifty.

Contrary to what many might believe (and what premillenialists suggest), the noun "tribulation" (*thlipsis*) is not just found in the book of Revelation, but is found 45 times in the New Testament. Its basic idea is "pressure" or "suffering." It is translated many ways in Scripture: tribulation, affliction, suffering, burdened, troubles, anguish, trial, etc. Our English word "tribulation" comes from the Latin term "tribulum"—the harrow or threshing instrument that separates the grain from its husk. It speaks of any hardship or persecution that we might endure. The question is, when will Christians experience hardship? Haven't all Christians (of all ages) been promised persecution?

In the book of Revelation, *"thlipsis"* occurs five times (1:9; 2:9, 10, 22; and 7:14). Notice that its first four uses are in reference to John himself (1:9) and the letters to the seven churches (2:9, 10, 22)—who were already undergoing "tribulation." The last reference in Revelation (7:14) actually speaks of those Christians who were martyred for their faith and had escaped the great tribulation. The great tribulation takes place on earth, and first century Christians were already experiencing it. Let me state that again: John and the Christians of his day were already going through the "tribulation."

Notice the following passages:

> "I have told you these things, so that in me you may have peace. In this world you will have trouble (tribulation, *thlipsis*). But take heart! I have overcome the world" (John 16:33).
>
> "Not only so, but we also rejoice in our sufferings (tribulation, *thlipsis*), because we know that suffering produces perseverance" (Romans 5:3).
>
> "You became imitators of us and of the Lord; in spite of severe suffering (tribulation, *thlipsis*), you welcomed the message with the joy given by the Holy Spirit" (1 Thessalonians 1:6).
>
> "Therefore, among God's churches we boast about your perseverance and faith in all the persecutions and trials (tribulation, *thlipsis*) you are enduring" (2 Thessalonians 1:4).

For Jesus and the New Testament writers, "tribulation" is the common lot of all the faithful. Christians have been, and will continue to be in the tribulation until set free by death or on the day Christ returns.

Bible references: Matthew 13:21; 24:9, 29; Mark 4:17; 13:19, 24; John 16:21; 16:33; Acts 7:10, 11; 11:19; 14:22; 20:23; Romans 2:9; 5:3 (2x); 8:35; 12:12; 1 Corinthians 7:28; 2 Corinthians 1:4 (2x), 1:8; 2:4; 4:17; 6:4; 7:4; 8:2, 13; Ephesians 3:13; Philippians 1:17; 4:14; Colossians 1:24; 1 Thessalonians 1:6; 3:3; 3:7; 2 Thessalonians 1:4, 6; Hebrews 10:33; James 1:27; Revelation 1:9; 2:9, 10, 22; 7:14.

EMAIL "Messages"

✉ INBOX [60/70]

To: Dr. Crane [eaglechristianchurch.com]
Subject: What about the Rapture?

---Original Message---

I have been reading the Left Behind *series. While I have enjoyed reading it, it has left me with many questions about the rapture. What am I to think?*

Reply:

The rapture of the church has captured the imagination of many in our generation. Proponents insist that "the church" will be removed from the world in a "secret coming" prior to the "second coming" of Christ. We have all seen the bumper stickers that read something to the effect, "In the event of the rapture, the driver of this vehicle will be taken." While the *Left Behind* series certainly has been popular, it might shock you to learn that the church knew nothing about a "rapture" prior to the 1800s when J. N. Darby and C. I. Scofield popularized this view.

First, I need to tell you dogmatically—an "invisible coming" of Jesus is not Scriptural. Furthermore, it should be stated that the word "rapture" is never even used in the Bible, and there is not one explicit verse to support such a position. Verses that have been used as justification have been twisted and contorted and when understood correctly, are either prophecies that have already been fulfilled (not waiting future fulfillment), or are simply descriptive of the once-and-for-all final coming of Jesus.

It might serve us well to answer a rather simple question: Why didn't Christians believe in a "rapture" until recently if this teaching were truly biblical? Even "rapturists" readily admit that their belief is not clearly articulated in Scripture, but a deduction from their overall system of theology.

The most common verse put forward by *Left Behind* theology is 1 Thessalonians 4:17. It speaks of believers being "caught up in the sky." They suggest that nonbelievers remain on earth—thus are "left behind." This passage actually refers to the second coming, not an invisible coming, and on that day every knee will bow and every tongue confess that Jesus Christ is Lord. There are no second chances. Even if it could be construed otherwise (no other details are given in this passage)—it would certainly not be enough to construct an elaborate, dogmatic, and specific teaching about a supposed rapture.

Actually, clear teachings of Scripture indicate that you WANT TO BE LEFT BEHIND! Let me reference two. The parable of the weeds (Matthew 13:24–30) suggests that the wicked will be judged prior to the wheat being gathered—not the other way around (the weeds are plucked out first)! Also, in the Olivet Discourse (Matthew 24:36–41), while some have suggested a "secret rapture," the climactic universal return of Christ is in view (24:27). In fact, the word "taken" in 24:40–41 (though a different verb in Greek) parallels "took" of 24:39 and suggests that those taken away are taken for eternal judgment (not "raptured"), while those left behind remain with Christ. The passage once again affirms that the unjust are taken in judgment while the righteous are left behind, not vice versa. The passage as a whole highlights the significance that no one knows when Christ will come back—we must constantly be ready.

The "rapture" teaching at its best is unbiblical and at its worst provides false hope—that people have another thousand years during which time they can accept or reject Jesus Christ as Savior.

EMAIL "Messages"

✉ INBOX [61/70]

To: Dr. Crane [eaglechristianchurch.com]
Subject: What Is the Mark of the Beast?

---Original Message---

Where does the number 666 come from and what exactly is the mark of the beast?

Reply:

In the book of Revelation, the number 666 stands for the mark of the beast and is said to be "a man's number" (Revelation 13:18). Many have attempted and failed to identify a specific person to whom this number might apply. I have heard speculations pointing to everyone from Hitler, Mussolini, Gorbachev, Kissinger, Reagan, Khadafi, Saddat, Bush, Bin Laden, Kim Jong-il, Castro, and now Obama. The truth is, it is possible to conclude that almost any human name, in some language, given some code, equals 666.

If any one human might be considered for this "honor," I might suggest that the Roman emperor Nero would fit the bill—for he was the epitome of evil at the time of the writing of the Book of Revelation. But even this identification does not capture the primary message given to us by the timeless Book of Revelation. Actually, those who insist on identifying a specific person, might miss the point of the passage entirely—that the beast gives his mark to people, and only those who receive the mark can buy or sell (13:17). The rest will be persecuted.

Let me first remind you that in the Book of Revelation, the followers of Christ have already been said to have been given a mark or seal (7:2–3). In chapter 13, the beast now gives his own mark.

While the mark of the beast is likely the most discussed aspect of the book of Revelation with many amusing answers given (freemasonry, the American dime, Sunday worship, credit cards, bar codes, international telephone numbers, etc.), the mark is not meant to be so complicated. The mark, like any brand, simply signifies that a slave belongs to his master. Here it seems to be directly related to who a person worships (20:4). The unbeliever is marked with 666 (the unholy trinity of six). I would posit that the believer could symbolically be marked with 777 (seven being considered to be the "complete" or "perfect" number). Don't forget, six is less than seven and never reaches seven. Six always fails to attain to perfection. Six means missing the mark or failure, while seven means completion or victory.

Symbolically then, we see all individuals receiving marks on their forehead and right hand (13:16). The forehead symbolizes the mind (Deuteronomy 6:8) and the right hand indicates deeds and actions. Therefore, receiving the mark indicates that the person (so characterized) belongs to the one he worships. In the context of this passage, only those who bear the mark of the beast will be able to buy or sell, while those who do not receive the mark of the beast will be persecuted by not being able to buy or sell. This type of persecution against Christians has certainly been true at times throughout history and will continue to happen until the "last day." One should remember, however, that the one who receives the mark of Christ (seal) will be victorious.

EMAIL "Messages"

✉ INBOX (62/70)

To: Dr. Crane [eaglechristianchurch.com]
Subject: What Is the Millennium?

---Original Message---

What is the Millennium?

Reply:

The word *millennium* is a Latin term that means one thousand years and is used to describe the events of Revelation chapter 20. Over the years there has been immense speculation and diverse interpretations regarding this passage. Most have read into John's account, ideas that come from other parts of the Bible (or are not found in the Bible) such as the rapture, the tribulation, or the reconstruction of the Jewish temple—none of which the Apostle John had in mind when writing. When it comes to the actual events of Revelation 20, most commentators fall into one of three basic schools of thought.

1. *Postmillennialists* believe that Christ will come *after* the Millennium has taken place. The kingdom of God will be extended in the world through the preaching of the gospel and the saving work of the Holy Spirit. Christ is already reigning through his obedient church, and will bring to the world a thousand years of peace and righteousness prior to his return at the conclusion of history.

2. *Premillennialists* believe that Christ will come *before* the Millennium begins. Despite all the efforts of Christians, society will continue to get worse and worse, and in the last days the Antichrist (see both emails about the last days and

the Antichrist) will gain control of human affairs—usually through government. Only the catastrophic return of Christ can inaugurate the golden age of one thousand years of peace here on earth.

3. *Amillennialsts* regard the thousand years, like other numbers in Revelation—as symbolic. Instead of being a literal period of exactly one thousand years, the expression refers to a very long time, extending from the first coming of Christ to his Second Coming. Thus, the church age is the Millennium and, therefore, we are in "the last days." During this entire period Satan's power is limited by the preaching of the gospel (Luke 10:18). The "last days" began with Jesus (Hebrews 1:2) and with the outpouring of the Holy Spirit on the day of Pentecost (Acts 2:16, 17), and they will end when the "last day" arrives (John 6:39, 40, 44, 54; 11:24; 12:48). Instead of the optimism of the postmillenarian or the pessimism of the premillenarian, the amillenarian takes seriously the realism of Jesus' parable of the weeds among the wheat (Matthew 13:24–30, 36–43); namely, that good and evil will develop side by side until the harvest, which is the end of the world.

See: *The Meaning of the Millennium: Four Views*, by Robert H. Clouse.

EMAIL "Messages"

✉ INBOX [63/70]

To: Dr. Crane [eaglechristianchurch.com]
Subject: Are There Warning Signs of the End of Time?

---Original Message---

Will there be any last-minute "warning signs" before Jesus returns?

Reply:

This question certainly highlights the popular, prevalent theological notion that before Christ returns there will be "wars and rumors of wars" (Matthew 24:6). However, a close examination of Scripture shows that most of the "signs" people refer to draw from Jesus' warning about the approaching judgment of Judaism (Matthew 23:29-36) and the destruction of Herod's Temple (Matthew 23:37—24:2) in A.D. 70. Jesus knew when that would be (Matthew 23:36; 24:34) and spoke of the imminent warning signs that could be seen by those heeding his warning. If they did so, they could escape from Judea (Matthew 24:15-16).

When Jesus speaks of his return, the illustrations actually point away from, rather than toward visible, last-minute warning signs. The illustrations he uses come upon man quickly. It will be like lightning (Matthew 24:27); like the days of Noah (Matthew 24:37-42); like a thief in the night (Matthew 24:43-44); like a master catching a lazy worker (Matthew 24:45-51); and like the appearance of the bridal party to the bridesmaids (Matthew 25:1-13). Jesus says quite clearly, "No one knows about that day or hour, not even the angels in heaven, nor the Son, but only the Father" (Matthew 24:36).

1 Thessalonians 5:2–3 says, "For you know very well that the day of the Lord will come like a thief in the night. While people are saying, 'Peace and safety,' destruction will come on them suddenly, as labor pains on a pregnant woman, and they will not escape."

For further reading see, *Marveling with Mark: A Homiletical Commentary on the Second Gospel,* 285.

EMAIL "Messages"

✉ INBOX [64/70]

To: Dr. Crane [eaglechristianchurch.com]
Subject: When Do People Go to Heaven?

---Original Message---

Some people tell me that when we die we go directly to heaven, but then I read that when Jesus comes again, God will create a new heaven and a new earth. If God has not yet created the new heaven, where do people go in the meantime? Can you straighten this out for me?

Reply:

The Bible tells us that when we die we will be absent from the body, but present with the Lord (2 Corinthians 5:8; Philippians 1:13). Many do refer to this as "going to heaven," some use the word "paradise" (Luke 23:43) to distinguish it from what heaven will be ultimately like, still others refer to this as an "intermediate state."

No matter what you call it—our physical bodies are dead, but our souls/spirits are with God until the second coming of Jesus, at which time the present heaven and earth will be destroyed and God will create a new heaven and a new earth (2 Peter 3:13; Revelation 21:1). At the second coming of Jesus, we will receive our new resurrected bodies.

Section Eight

Objections to Christianity

EMAIL "Messages"

✉ INBOX [65/70]

To: Dr. Crane [eaglechristianchurch.com]
Subject: Aren't All Religions Basically the Same?

---Original Message---

I was talking to a friend about Christianity, but he seems to think that all of the religions of the world are basically the same. For example, he says that all the religions believe in God—they just have different names. I know we covered this in our 401 class at ECC, but I can't remember how to respond.

Reply:

I would probably admit that on the surface, it might appear that way—much like a cubic zirconia and a diamond might appear identical. Cubic zirconia is the cubic crystalline form of zirconium dioxide. The synthesized material is hard, optically flawless and looks like a diamond—but I wouldn't suggest giving one to your bride-to-be. If a person takes only a cursory look at the major religions of the world they might find certain similarities between them regarding a belief in God, a code of ethics, and a way of enlightenment. But similarities in one respect can hardly equate to sameness on the whole. A quick glance in any book on various world religions will reveal major differences—even diametrically opposed views on essential elements.

Take, for instance, your friend's statement that all the different religions just use "different names for God." While it is true that different religions have different names for God (Brahman, Allah, Kami, Shang Ti, Dainichi), there is more at stake than just the name. For example, take three of the world's major religions:

Buddhism, Hinduism, and Christianity. Each of these holds to a view of God that is mutually exclusive (unable to both be true at the same time). Many forms of Buddhism don't believe there is a God. Hinduism teaches that everything that exists is a part of God. Christianity teaches that God exists, but that he is separate from everything else that he created. It is an absurdity to suggest that these three views about God are compatible, much less equal. Furthermore, of those religions that do actually believe that God exists, their specific views about his character and nature are also mutually exclusive.

Similarly, many religions make faith claims about Jesus. Islam, for example, holds Jesus out to be a prophet from God (not unlike many of the prophets found in our Old Testament). Some mystics call him a great teacher. Others claim him to be a pioneer, a trailblazer, or an example. But Christianity proclaims Jesus Christ to be God incarnate—God in the flesh. And only Jesus backs up his claim to authority by physically rising from the dead.

Most importantly, the Bible is not silent about this issue. In both the Old and New Testaments, we find other religions simultaneously in existence, and they were never perceived to be "basically the same," or viewed as acceptable alternatives.

The truth of the matter is, all religions make truth claims which make them different—and truth, by definition, is mutually exclusive. Only one of them (or none of them) can be true. But even more than when purchasing a diamond, with something of this magnitude, you would do well to shop carefully.

See: Numbers 25:3–5; 1 Kings 18:16–40; and 1 Corinthians 10:20.

EMAIL "Messages"

✉ INBOX [66/70]

To: Dr. Crane [eaglechristianchurch.com]
Subject: What about All of Christianity's Injustice?

---Original Message---

If Christianity is true, why is it responsible for so much evil and injustice in the world? Aren't Christians just another group of religious fanatics?

Reply:

Any amount of violence, evil, or injustice done in the name of Christianity is a terrible calamity for which there is no excuse. But if violence, evil, and injustice have been done in the name of Christianity, they have been done not because the people involved were overly committed to the gospel of Jesus Christ, but because they were not committed enough to it. Atrocities have happened, but they have never been condoned by true Christ-followers. Christianity at its very core is about loving God and loving others—even loving our enemies. Christianity is not about evil and injustice, but about the abolition of evil and injustice through Christ Jesus.

Actually (although I hear this argument often), the claim that Christianity is the cause of great injustice against humanity is at best, greatly exaggerated, and at worst, a blatant falsifying of the evidence. When dealing with this issue, four topics of discussion usually surface: the Crusades, the Inquisition, the Salem Witch Trials, and anti-abortion gunmen. Let me take each in turn.

The Crusades are often cited to illustrate the horrors of Christianity. But is it true? We should start by remembering that before the rise of Islam, the Middle East was predominantly Christian. Inspired by Islam's call to jihad, Muhammad's armies conquered Jerusalem and the entire Middle East, turning churches into mosques. Muslims laid siege to parts of Africa, Asia, and then moved north into Europe. The Crusades were a rallying cry of the people to fight back. Not all of the Crusaders were Christian, nor were they funded by the church—they were people who were trying to regain their land from the oppressors.

During the first Crusade, Jerusalem was recaptured and held for many years. Islam was held at bay temporarily. Many historians have noted that without the Crusades, Western Civilization might have been completely overrun by the forces of Islam and what you are now reading would need to be written in Arabic. In the history of warfare, there is no warrant for considering the Crusades anything but an attempt of a embattled people group to defend themselves from foreign conquest.

As far as the Inquisition, historians have now established that the horrific images of the Inquisition are largely a myth and the few crimes that actually occurred cannot be attributed primarily to Christians. During a period of more than 350 years, it is now estimated that about 2,000 people were killed. These deaths are all tragic, but that is fewer than six people per year. This hardly be described as an atrocity at the hands of the church.

The best example of religiously motivated violence in America by Christians is the Salem Witch Trials. From the way people talk, you might assume that hundreds, thousands, or even tens of thousands of people were sentenced to death and killed during this period of American history. While doing my Doctorate in Massachusetts, I went to see the location of these trials. Do you know how many people were actually killed as a result of these trials? Nineteen!

As for abortion-clinic gunmen, someone needs to explain to me the thought process of a person who says we need to save a life by shooting another. All of mainstream Christianity stands repulsed by such acts of violence. Christianity teaches that we are to love all people—even those who don't agree with us! Let me say again, if violence, evil, and injustice have been done in the name of Christianity, it has been done, not because the people involved were overly committed to the gospel of Jesus Christ, but because they were not committed enough to it.

Actually, it would be telling to compare these numbers to the atrocities done by those who opposed Christianity in favor of scientific atheism. In the past hundred years, powerful communist governments have wiped out over twenty million people. Mao Zedong's regime in China accounts for about seventy million deaths. Hitler comes in a distant third with around ten million murders—most of them Jews, but many Christians.

We could add to that list thousands more by including some "lesser" atheist tyrants: Pol Pot, Enver Hoxha, Nicolae Ceausescu, Fidel Castro, Kim Jong-il. It is the atheist regimes that are responsible for the mass evil that has happened. In a single century they have murdered more than one hundred million people.

Simply put, Christianity is not the source of great injustice in the world. Dinesh D'Souza in his book *What's So Great About Christianity?* says, "The indisputable fact is that all the religions of the world put together have in three thousand years not managed to kill anywhere near the number of people killed in the name of atheism in the past few decades. It's time to abandon the mindless repeated mantra that religious belief has been the main source of human conflict and violence" (221). Atheism, not religion (especially not Christianity), is responsible for the evil and injustice in history.

EMAIL "Messages"

✉ INBOX [67/70]

To: Dr. Crane [eaglechristianchurch.com]
Subject: Isn't Christianity Narrow-minded?

---Original Message---

Isn't it narrow-minded for Christians to think that they are right and everyone else is wrong?

Reply:

I need to start by stating a principle of reality: truth by definition is exclusive—if something is true it excludes those statements or principles that are false. Everyone who believes in a particular "truth" excludes those statements or principles that are in disagreement with that "truth." The real question is: Is it really narrow-minded for someone to choose truth over falsehood? I would suggest that it is foolish (not narrow-minded) for someone to reject the truth in an attempt to hold to other options that are not true.

Let me set theology aside for a moment. If you were suffering from a very treatable disease, would it be narrow-minded for you to accept the proven medicine your family doctor prescribes to help treat your illness? Would wisdom lead you to follow this course of action over many other possible options? After all, there are other alternative remedies! You could consult a tribal witch doctor who might use lizard lips and chicken gizzards. You could call the 1-800 psychic hotline and find a psychic healer who could consult the galactic universe as to the cause of your illness. There are some who might suggest that your ailment is simply psychosomatic—what you need to do is cleanse your mind of bad thoughts. Others would suggest it is simply your bad "karma" catching up with you and you should accept your fate.

Is it narrow-minded to choose your doctor's advice over these many other options? No! Wisdom often leads us to follow a certain course of action over another. The real question is not "are we being narrow-minded?" but, "who has the credentials you trust?" Hands down, I'm choosing my M.D. over lizard-gizzards!

Christianity is no different. After an examination of all the facts, I am convinced that the Bible is accurate and that Jesus is indeed the Son of God. I believe Jesus came to earth, lived as a man, and died for our sins to provide reconciliation with God. If I have become convinced of "the truth" of Jesus, must I not also believe his words when he says, "I am the way and the truth and the life. No one comes to the Father except through me" (John 14:6)?

The question is not whether Christianity is "narrow-minded." The question is whether or not I have good reason to accept my position over all of the other options. I have done my homework and am convinced! Christianity proves itself trustworthy in ways that other religions and viewpoints do not! Actually, when I find someone condemning my belief as being exclusive—that person, at that moment, is doing the very thing they are condemning in me by condemning my belief! They are excluding my answer as a legitimate option. Isn't that narrow-minded?

One last thing. Avoid confusing truth and tolerance—they are two very different things. I will hold strongly to what I believe and communicate it clearly, while at the same time supporting the rights of others to disagree with my viewpoint.

EMAIL "Messages"

✉ INBOX [68/70]

To: Dr. Crane [eaglechristianchurch.com]
Subject: Isn't Religion Culturally Conditioned?

---Original Message---

We are all products of the culture we grew up in. The reason people are Christian, or Hindu, or Buddhist is because of where they are born and the cultural influences. Isn't it true that you were born to Christian parents? What if you were born in Pakistan? Cultural influences would have made you Muslim.

Reply:

One of the most popular objections to Christianity I used to hear was that all religions are equally true. Today, however, I am more likely to be told that all religions are equally false. The objection goes like this: "All religious claims are simply the product of your particular historical and cultural moment. No one can claim they can know the truth, since no one can judge whether one assertion about a spiritual reality is truer than another." This seems to be at the heart of your email.

While it is true (to some extent) that we are products of our cultural upbringing, and while this can make evaluating competing truth-claims harder, is it really a foregone conclusion that we are then unable to weigh the rightness or wrongness of competing belief systems?

Cultural relativism (or in some cases pluralism) not only suggests that we are all products of our culture, but maintains that "no belief can be held universally true for everyone." The problem with

Objections to Christianity 171

such a statement is that it in itself is a comprehensive claim about everyone that is the product of social conditions—so it cannot be true on its own terms. It is a self-refuting argument.

Even then, suppose I were to concede that if I had been born of Muslim parents in Pakistan (rather than Christian parents in Oregon) my beliefs would be quite different. And, suppose I were to concede that if a Muslim born in Pakistan had been born in the U. S. to Christian parents his beliefs might be different. Shouldn't I also concede that if a cultural relativist was also born in Pakistan to Muslim parents he probably wouldn't be a cultural relativist? Here, too, we find a self-refuting argument.

Yes, we are all to some extent products of our culture. But you cannot say, "All claims about religions are culturally conditioned except the one I am making right now!" If you insist that no one can determine which beliefs are right and wrong, why should I believe what you are saying?

The truth is, while we all make truth-claims, and while it might be a challenge to separate our truth claims from the culture in which we were raised, we still have the ability and the responsibility to weigh carefully and critical what we believe and why. Truth exists outside of our cultural ethos.

EMAIL "Messages"

✉ INBOX [69/70]

To: Dr. Crane [eaglechristianchurch.com]
Subject: Isn't Sincerely Believing Enough?

---Original Message---

I appreciate the sincerity in which you preach. But many other "faiths" sincerely believe their message as well. If a person really believes, does it really make any difference what they believe?

Reply:

Let me begin by saying, I do truly believe what I preach—but that doesn't make it right! What makes something right is whether or not it is true. Many have sincerely believed in something only to have been sincerely wrong.

This is true in all areas of life. Sincerely believing it is safe to cross the street doesn't help you if there is traffic coming. Sincerely believing the speed limit is 65 when in reality it is 45 won't prevent you from getting a traffic ticket for speeding. Sincerely believing that a foot-bridge is strong enough to hold you has no impact if the planks are rotten or the ropes are frayed. Likewise, strongly holding to your beliefs about God does not make them true.

What counts is not the sincerity of our faith, but the object of our faith. Weak faith in a strong bridge does not lesson its capacity, nor does strong faith in a weak bridge give it any further stability. What is truly important is the actual strength of the bridge. The amount of one's faith has no effect on reality. What is important is not the amount of our faith as much as it is the object of our faith. Here is what we need to ask: Is what I'm believing in—believable? Is what I'm trusting in—trustworthy?

We need to listen to the advice given to us in Scripture: "Test everything. Hold on to the good" (1 Thessalonians 5:21). Let's make sure we do our homework and believe things because they are true.

EMAIL "Messages"

✉ INBOX [70/70]

To: Dr. Crane [eaglechristianchurch.com]
Subject: What about the Problem of Evil?

---Original Message---

If an all-loving and all-powerful God really exists, why doesn't he do something about all of the evil in the world?

Reply:

This is a difficult question and one that I still struggle with at times. It is perhaps the most often cited reason given by atheists for their disbelief in God. It is certainly not a new question. It dates back at least to Epicurus (a Greek philosopher from the fourth century B.C.) who asked, "Is God willing to prevent evil, but not able? Then he is impotent. Is he able, but not willing? Then he is malevolent. Is he both able and willing? Whence then is evil?"

The idea (given the presence of evil) is: if God is good—he is not powerful, or, if he is powerful—he is not good. God couldn't be both powerful and good since evil continues in the world. Therefore, the God of Christianity does not exist.

But this objection to the existence of God hinges on a mistaken premise. It assumes that a good God would not allow evil to continue. The reasoning goes like this: we cannot think of any justifiable reason why a good God would allow suffering and evil, therefore, God cannot have a good reason!

Is it possible that God has a reason that we have not thought of?

Actually, I believe God is an all-powerful God who can and will put an end to all evil, but the reason he has not done so (yet) is precisely because he is all-loving! If God were to immediately destroy all evil—he would have to start with me because I am part of the problem—there is evil in me. I suspect that if God decided to get rid of all evil, he would have to destroy you as well!

One day God will put an end to evil, but he hasn't done so because he is waiting. Why is God waiting? Because we matter to him. God's delay is because he wants more people to turn to him, and sometimes that only happens through pain and suffering! Pain (although not necessarily caused by God) is his megaphone. Peter says, "God is patient with you, not wanting anyone to perish, but everyone to come to repentance" (2 Peter 3:9).

Contrary to what some think, the existence of evil should lead us toward God rather than away from him. If there were no God, there would be no standard for right and wrong—life would simply be "chance" and "survival of the fittest." If that were the case, there would be no meaning or moral value. The very moment that someone protests that they have been wronged or that life is unfair, they have betrayed their belief in a standard that is ultimately above all of us—a standard that did not come from us, but from the One who made us.

One last thing. The Bible actually tells us that God sent Jesus to suffer and die for us. You might think that the presence of evil in the world means that God doesn't care. No! The cross of Christ speaks loudly—God's own son suffered evil out of his love for you.

BIBLIOGRAPHY

Ankerberg, John, and John Weldon. *Ready with an Answer.* Eugene: Harvest House, 1997.
Cottrell, Jack. *The Authority of the Bible.* Grand Rapids: Baker, 1978.
Crane, Steven A. *Marveling with Mark: A Homiletical Commentary on the Second Gospel.* Eugene: Wipf & Stock, 2010.
D'Souza, Dinesh. *What's So Great About Christianity.* Washington D.C.: Regnery, 2007.
Fee, Gordon D. and Douglas Stuart. *How to Read the Bible Book by Book.* Grand Rapids: Zondervan, 2002.
Geisler, Norman, and Ron Brooks. *When Skeptics Ask.* Grand Rapids: Baker Books, 1990.
Geisler, Norman, and Thomas Howe. *When Critics Ask.* Wheaton, IL: Victor Books, 1992.
Geisler, Norman L., and Frank Turek. *I Don't Have Enough Faith to be an Atheist.* Wheaton: Crossway Books, 2004.
Keller, Timothy. *The Reason for God.* New York: Riverhead Books, 2008.
Lightfoot, Neil R. *How We Got the Bible.* Grand Rapids: Baker Books, 2009.
McDowell, Josh. *More than a Carpenter.* Wheaton, IL: Living Books, 1973.
Mears, Henrietta. *What the Bible Is All About.* Ventura, CA: Regal Books, 1997.
Morris, Leon. *Jesus Is the Christ: Studies in the Theology of John.* Grand Rapids: Eerdmans, 1989.
Sanders, J. Oswald. *How Lost Are the Heathen.* Chicago: Moody Press, 1966.
Strobel, Lee. *The Case for Christ.* Grand Rapids: Zondervan, 1998.
———. *The Case for Faith.* Grand Rapids: Zondervan, 2000.
———. *The Case for the Real Jesus.* Grand Rapids: Zondervan, 2007.

www.ingramcontent.com/pod-product-compliance
Lightning Source LLC
Chambersburg PA
CBHW050805160426
43192CB00010B/1649